MAZEPA The Great
Cossack & Hetman of the Ukraine
The Origin of Ethnic Cleansing

By Dr. S. C. Mazepa

MAZEPA THE GREAT COSSACK
&
HETMAN OF THE UKRAINE
THE ORIGIN OF ETHNIC CLEANSING

This edition published in 1995 by
MAZEPA Publishing
3305 West Emmaus Ave.
Emmaus, PA 18049 U.S.A.
(610) 797-4800

Author, Editor, Artwork, Publisher: Dr. S. C. Mazepa

Printed in the U.S.A

Dedicated to my father,
Stephen A. Mazepa
and in living memory to
my mother,
Ruth G. Mazepa

Dr. S. C. Mazepa

Acknowledgements:

JACOB ABBOTT
Peter the Great - 1859

EUGENE SCHUYLER
Peter the Great - 1890

LORD BYRON
Mazepa - 1818

NISHET BAIN
Charles XII of Sweden - 1895

A.S. PUSHKIN
Poltava - 1827

TSCHAIKOVSKY
Peter Ilich - 1840-93

VICTOR HUGO
Marie - Playwriter
1802-85

FRANZ LISZT
Composer of Mazepa
1811-86

PREFACE

This book is a translation in the first writings of the History of Russia and the Ukraine, used in the early years of WWII for the Soviet secondary school system abandoned after being prepared by the Institute of History of the U.S.S.R. Academy of Sciences, never completed and or released. Now that the Soviet Union doesn't exist, the story of a revisionist point of view can be written using their valuable untapped research and resources, compiled in a derivative style and for easy reading. I tried to start out using small chapters to keep it interesting, as the story flows into the origins of Ukrainian statehood, and a United Ukrainian independent state. These ideals, I myself, have inherited from my Ukrainian ancestors. I received this heritage from my father as a young man and from his predecessors. I will never forget as a young boy before going to bed each night my father would say to me, "Remember my son, you are Ukrainian, not Russian, and a day will come in your lifetime that you will contribute to your Ukrainian heritage and to future Ukrainian generations not yet born". This book relieves me of this life-long burden.

Mazepa's era constituted the beginning of the birth of the Ukraine. He consolidated Ukrainian lands of the Ukraine, and established a Hetman regime of a European style.

He considered coexistence with Moscow in a two-pronged policy when necessary for the attainment of his political objectives, and whenever it was possible to do so. Mazepa was motivated by a deep dedication to the interest of the Ukraine and from his love for his own country.

Mazepa knew he had to break with Moscow, which led to armed conflict. He depended totally on the Swedish victory, which never happened. He was labeled "Father of the Ukrainian Independence", and hated by all Russians, both Red Communists in our century and Imperial Russia of the last 250 years.

They failed to defeat Mazepa as a spiritual spokesman of Ukrainian Nationalism. It failed to defeat and destroy him. The

Ukraine has survived over 280 years of Russian slavery and it's rebirth today is much stronger ideologically because it now knows the name Mazepa is a symbol for Ukrainian Independence in the 21st Century, to be a member of the family of free nations and interact in free trade with the free world. The Ukraine has all the resources to become self-sufficient. In the words of my father and his fathers, "Freedom for the Ukraine forever someday".

As the year 2000 approaches, it's easy to forget the past histories never spoken in our times. "Mazepa the Great Cossack - Hetman of the Ukraine", focuses on the past, present and future. The Ukraine, a sleeping giant, with the potential for a role-model play in the next century, can only go forward in it's independence, if it learns from it's past.

Great writers, poets and composers and playwrights remind us of a lost reality. Lord Byron's poem of 1818, Mazepa, Pushkin's poem of 1827, Poltava, Tschaikovsky and Liszt's compositions of Mazepa, Victor Hugo's play Mazepa, etc., cannot be ignored. Time has passed these great men on to the ages. One thing they, like other great movers and shakers of their day, had in common is that they were all moved by Mazepa.

This book is a romantic essay for the revival of the reduction of boredom. I tried to include every interest of the readers. Historians, music, poets, military, political, economical and the down to earth realist, are the readers I'd like to stir. Starting from day one, several thousands of years ago up to Mazepa's time and even today, the story flows from fast moving short chapters to longer ones as the story unfolds. I designed the book size and type to fit into any overcoat, briefcase, or pocket book. The type used will allow you to read it without glasses. The paper non-reflective. I decided a long time to do this book in memory of my father and mother. But to do it right, to write, edit and publish with complete independence from outside influences that dictate style, form and input. Even the dust cover was completely independent of outside influence. For the first time in our lifetime, the yoke of suppression has been broken from the Russians. We welcome the Ukrainian nation to the family of free and democratic nations of the free world. I hope you enjoy "Mazepa the Great Cossack - Hetman of the Ukraine, as much as I did in writing it.

Dr. S. C. Mazepa

"The Ukraine shall not die, but shall live on forever free".

Ivan Stephanovich Mazepa 1695
Dr. Stephen C. Mazepa 1995

CONTENTS

CHAPTER 1

THE PRIMITIVE COMMUNITY SYSTEM IN THE UKRAINE

PRIMEVAL SOCIETY
THE BIRTH OF UKRAINIAN SOCIETY

The first traces of human life in Europe date back to that distant period when the climate was warm and humid. The luxuriant, ever-green forests consisted of laurel, box, yew and other species of trees. The woods and riverbanks abounded in animals which today are either extinct (as the prehistoric elephant, and a peculiar genus of rhinoceros) or which now occur only in southern lands (as the hippo-potamus and leopard).

Human beings lived in small groups ("primitive hordes"). The first implements used by man were rough-chipped stones. People ob-tained their food in common by gathering snails, insects, fruit and edible roots. The hunting of small animals was still a casual pursuit. Because of the warm climate man had no need for the protection of special shelters or clothing.

The earliest squatting places of man in Russia are those discovered in the Caucasus (near Sukhumi) and in the Crimea. A large number of split animal bones and crude stone implements have been found in caves not far from Simferopol. These were the dwell-ings of primitive hunters who used natural caves as protection against beasts and as shelter in time of bad weather.

Life led to the formation of the primitive community. Every-thing, with the exception of some insignificant articles, belonged to the community; private property did not yet exist. In the primitive community there were no rich and poor, no exploitation of man by man. Productive forces were very poorly developed.

People learned to make mud-huts and hovels as a shelter

from the cold. Not long ago the remains of such a dwelling place were dis-covered on the Don River, near the village of Gagarino. The bottom of the hut was a shallow, oval pit the sides of which were lined with boulders and large bones, to which poles were affixed, joined together at the top and forming a roof covered with twigs and hides. The bones of the mammoth, rhinoceros, bull and various small animals were found scattered inside the hut. Ornaments were also discovered there—the teeth of small beasts of prey, shells, and several carved bone figures of women.

As many as 200 habitats of ancient human society have been discovered. They are scattered in various places in the south-ern half of the European territory, in the Altai Mountains and in Western and Eastern Siberia, and are evidence of the profound antiquity of human society in Russia.

CHAPTER 2

ORIGIN OF THE MATRIARCHAL CLAN

As the climate changed, the vast glaciers vanished. They remained only in the extreme north and on mountain peaks. Gradually the conditions of nature became more like what they are today. The animal world changed; many large beasts, such as the mammoth and the cave lion, became extinct. Man's struggle for existence was considerably mitigated.

The primitive community had had no definite social organi-zation and readily disintegrated. On the other hand, the existence of a common economy called for a more stable and permanent social organi-zation.

In the course of many thousands of years people handed down from generation to generation acquired labor habits. They learned to make implements of various sizes and shape from flint and bone, such as axes, hammers, knives, celts, picks, spear points, etc. They started polishing the surfaces of the stone implements, making them easier to handle. People learned to sharpen and pierce stones and fix them onto handles. Of great importance was the

2

appearance of the bow and arrow which enabled the hunter to kill his quarry from afar.

His new production technique enabled man to rise to a higher stage of human civilization, that of barbarism. Man began to make earthenware, which was necessary for storing water, especially in dry regions. At first, the uten-sils were made of wood, twigs and skins. Then, to make them more durable, the walls of the wooden vessels were lined with clay. Still later the entire vessel was made of clay alone. Finally, the potter's wheel appeared, and with it pottery production. The plait-ing of baskets from twigs and rushes anticipated the weaving of the fibre of wild plants. This was the beginning of textile production. Coarse, hand-woven fabric was used for clothing, bags, and the like. Man's vocations became more intricate and diverse. He began to use nets woven of fibre for fishing. His chief hunting weapons were the spear, the harpoon, and the bow and arrow. During their excavations, archeologists sometimes find the bones of large beasts of prey with flint arrowheads deeply imbedded in them.

Primitive agriculture, which was carried on chiefly by the women, provided mankind with a more stable economic basis. Gradually, in the course of centuries, primitive people began to revere woman as the symbol of fertility. Realizing the importance of maternity, they also honored woman as the ancestral Mother. And woman, as the Mother, tiller of the soil, and guardian of the life of the group, became head of the primitive matriarchal clan.

When a man took a wife, he went to live with her clan, where he was subordinate to his wife's mother. At clan meetings, woman, the Mother, was in command, and members of the clan honored only their female ancestors. For the murder of or insult to one of their kin, the entire clan sought revenge. Inter-clan blood feuds became endless wars. For purposes of war several clans joined to form tribes. Clans consisted of several hundred people, and were united chiefly for work. A tribe combined a number of clans comprising several thousand people, who primarily formed a military group. At tribal meetings the armed people—men and women—elected leaders and elders, and decided questions of war and peace. Women were also tribal chieftains.

The men, who were hunters, tamed wild animals. This laid the foundation for animal herding. The first domestic animal was the dog. In northern regions man tamed the reindeer.

CHAPTER 3

HABITATIONS OF CLAN COMMUNITIES

Many dwelling places of clan communities have been found all over the Ukraine, from the shores of the Black Sea and the valleys of the Transcaucasian Mountains to the Far North, and from Byelorussia to Eastern Siberia. This material has enabled scientists to determine how people lived in that remote epoch.

In the forest belt people lived along riverbanks and lake shores. Each settlement belonged to a single clan and consisted of a few hovels. The dwellers' chief occupation was fishing, and to some extent hunting. In some places clan settlements were located in groups, a fact that points to the rise of a tribal union of clans.

In the south, where the country consisted of mixed forest and steppeland, and especially in the fertile river valleys, the chief occupation of the population was tilling the ground with the hoe. As an example of a primitive agricultural society we have the Tripolye civilization, relics of which were first discovered near the village of Tripolye (not far from Kiev). Numerous settlements of the Tripolye civilization have been found on Ukrainian territory, west of the Dnieper; they are said to be about 6,000 years old.

Settlements were located on high banks or on the slopes of ravines at the bottom of which streams flowed. The site selected for a dwelling was spread with clay which was baked hard with the help of bonfires. The walls were built of piles and sticks coated with clay. The result was a fairly spacious dwelling with several hearths inside. These crudely constructed houses accommodated up to a hundred and more people. The people planted wheat, barley and millet not far from their place of abode. Wooden flint-tipped hoes were used to turn up the soil. The grain was ground between large stone slabs.

A large number of clay statuettes of animals have been found; a magical power was presumably ascribed to these statuettes which were supposed to protect the domestic herd and help it to multiply. Pictures of domestic animals are also to be found on vessels.

Occasionally articles made of copper are found in the villages of the Tripolye civilization. Little casting moulds have been unearthed, pointing to the fact that some of these articles were made at the place where they were found. The frequent occurrence of metallic objects coincides with the period when the matriarchal clan system began to decline.

CHAPTER 4

THE PATRIARCHAL CLAN & THE DEVELOPMENT OF HERDING

The domestication of wild animals was of great importance in the life of the clan communities. Possessing domestic animals, people had a constant supply of food and were no longer dependent on the outcome of their hunt, which was not always a success. The taming of dogs and reindeer (in the north) was followed by the domestication of other animals such as cattle, goats, sheep, swine and horses. Gradually herding became the chief pursuit of the community. At first the cattle lived all year by grazing near the settlement. Later the people began to make hay as fodder for the winter; in the north thin leafy twigs were dried and shredded for this purpose. During the winter domestic animals lived in the same houses with the people. Later special sheds were put up for the animals. Large herds of cattle could not remain in one place for a great length of time. People therefore began to migrate with their cattle in search of fresh pasturage. Thus, nomad herding originated in the vast steppeland. Dairy farming, and the making of cheese and butter appeared with the development of cattle raising. Man learned to treat the wool of animals and to spin thread from it; then he began to make warm fabrics which were a good protection against the cold. Later the weaving loom was invented.

The breeding of domestic animals enabled man to use them in turning up the soil. This led to the appearance of the first tilling implement—the wooden plough. The first primitive plough was probably a tree limb with a bent, pointed bough or rhizome.

CHAPTER 5

ORIGIN OF THE PATRIARCHAL CLAN

Herding was the chief occupation of the man. It greatly enhanced his importance in the community. Man, the livestock breeder, replaced woman in agriculture: he tilled the land with the aid of animals (the bull, deer and horse) and freed woman from heavy physical labor with the hoe or plough. By using draft animals, man transformed hoe agriculture into plough farming. Kinship began to be traced from the male line, and no longer from the female. The matriarchal clan, which had existed heretofore, disappeared, and was replaced by the patriarchal clan, that is, a union of relatives who originated from a common male ancestor.

It became the established custom for a man's children to inherit their father's property, and this led to the accumulation of wealth in the family. Rich families began to withdraw from the clan. This accelerated the disintegration of the primitive community system.

CHAPTER 6

DEVELOPMENT OF COPPER AND BRONZE AGE CULTURE

The most ancient copper articles found on the territory of Russia date back to 3,000 B.C. They were originally introduced from southern and eastern lands. Local production came into being no later than 2,000 B.C. The mountains of the Caucasus, Central Asia, the Altai and the Urals became seats of the Bronze Age civilization. From here the use of bronze implements spread to the steppe and forest regions.

The inhabitants of the European forest belts and the vast wooded areas of Siberia remained preeminently hunters and fisherman. They lived in small villages far removed from each other.

The primitive community system still prevailed there. In the grassy plains of Southern Siberia, Central Asia and the Black Sea regions, herding became the basic occupation. Agriculture predominated in the fertile valleys. Here the disintegration of the primitive community proceeded more rapidly. Communities of husbandmen and herders developed more quickly than communities of hunters.

Numerous tumuli are scattered throughout the Southern Black Sea steppes, which, when excavated, revealed human skeletons dyed a red color. During burial, the dead body was covered with ochre or minimum (read lead), which later settled in the bones. The dead man's weapons and various household chattels were placed beside him. Sometimes the skeletons of a man and a woman were found together in the same burial mound. It is to be presumed that when a man, the head of a family, died, his wife was killed and buried with him. The barrows reveal that there were rich and poor burials, and testify to the incidence of inequality in property status. An example of an especially lavish burial that of a clan or a tribal chief—is the tumulus discovered near the city of Maikop. The mound was about 30 feet high. The main section of the sepulchre contained a skeleton which had been colored a bright red with minium. The deceased was dressed in clothing ornamented with golden images of bulls, rings, rosettes, and also with gold, cornelian and turquoise beads, and other small objects. Gold and silver vessels lay beside him. A canopy had been erected above the body, and was supported on gold and silver tubular piles decorated with solid gold and silver figures of bulls. The grave contained two other skeletons in special sections; the chieftain's nearest relatives had to die with him.

The Bronze Age flourished during the second millennium and the beginning of the first millennium B.C. in the mountains of the Caucasus, Transcaucasia and the Altai. Ancient mines from which ore was obtained for the local production of bronze, have been discovered in many places.

CHAPTER 7

BEGINNING OF THE IRON AGE

Iron objects appeared on the territory of the Ukraine at the end of the second millennium B.C. At first iron was used to ornament bronze articles. In the first half of the first millennium B.C. the production of iron implements had already originated in various places, and these articles began to replace bronze weapons and tools. By the middle of the first millennium B.C. iron had firmly established itself in the life of the population of our country. It increased the productivity of labor tremendously, especially in agriculture and the crafts. Iron made possible agriculture on a larger scale and the clearing of extensive forest tracts for cultivation; it gave the craftsman a tool of such hardness and sharpness that no stone, no other known metal, could withstand it.

The beginning of the first millennium B.C. witnessed the birth of a class society in the southern mountains of Transcaucasia and in Asia Minor. The iron ploughshare and the iron ax brought about the decline of the primitive community system.

CHAPTER 8

EARLIEST SLAVEOWNING STATES
IN THE CAUCASUS AND CENTRAL ASIA

In the primitive community oppression did not exist. With the development of herding, agriculture and domestic crafts, men were able to produce more than was necessary for their own subsistence. This led to the accumulation of stocks and the bartering of products among the clan communities. With the development of private family ownership of the means of production, individual families also engaged in inter-family barter. Such barter further stimulated production, which would no longer be maintained by the labor power of a single family or clan.

Wars furnished a new source of labor power: prisoners of war were no longer killed, but were converted into slaves. War was now waged for the sake of capturing prisoners no less than for that of plunder. Wars still further increased property inequality. The rich could enslave not only people of alien tribes, but also their own tribesmen and clansmen. Thus arose a division of society into classes: a class of slaveowners and a class of slaves. The slaveowner considered his slaves his absolute property, just as he did any other article that belonged to him. He could sell, buy and kill his slave just as he did his cattle. A slave had no property of his own. His labor was extensively employed in the economy. The condition of slaves was a very wretched one, yet compared to the primitive community, the system of slavery was a progressive stage.

CHAPTER 9

FORMATION OF THE SLAVEOWNING STATE

The state came into being with the development of property and inequality. It was essential to the propertied class as a means of preserving amassed riches and maintaining its power over the slaves and the indigent population. The body politic arose on the ruins of the primitive community system.

With the appearance of property inequality, clan and tribal chieftains came to be elected from among the rich families. Wars of plunder enriched these chieftains still further and made them more powerful; with them their military retinues also enriched themselves. These retinues helped to make the rule of the chiefs hereditary. A special armed force, one which replaced the former tribal volunteer levy, was required to keep the slaves and poor in subjection. Popular justice was replaced by a new court of law, one which served the interests of the ruling minority. In the clan, society had been governed according to traditional customs. Laws that protected the interests of the slaveowners appeared in the slaveowning state. A state power unknown under the primitive community system was formed in this manner.

Ancient states expanded by subjugating weaker neighboring tribes. Such multi-tribal states were unstable since they were founded not on economic ties but on the power of the conqueror. They therefore united or fell apart according to the success or failure of one or another military leader or ruler.

CHAPTER 10

ANCIENT TRANSCAUCASIAN STATES

The first slaveowning state to appear on the territory originated in Transcaucasia near Assyria. In the middle of the second millennium B.C. the mountainous land in the region of the triple lakes, Van, Sevan and Urmiya, and the upper reaches of the Tigris and Euphrates rivers and their tributaries, was occupied by small tribal unions. The Assyrian kings undertook frequent campaigns against them. This country of the triple lakes was named Urartu (Urardhu) by the Assyrian kings.

In the beginning of the first millennium B.C. the small principalities of Urartu united under the supremacy of the stronger tribes. The united tribes, called Chaldeans—after the name of their god, Chaldu (Khaldu)—formed a kingdom headed by powerful rulers, who not only effectively repelled the attacks of the Assyrians, but themselves launched campaigns against them. A capital which was well protected in the south by the Iranian Mountain Range was built on the shore of Lake Van (near the present city of Van). During the 9th-8th B.C. centuries before our era the dominions of Urartu expanded tremendously.

To commemorate their victories the kings of Urartu left cuneiform inscriptions on rocks and cliffs, which were sometimes located in very inaccessible places. These writings, telling of important events in the history of Urartu, have been deciphered with great difficulty by Russian and foreign scientists.

The kingdom of Urartu attained its maximum size and power in the middle of the 8th century B.C. In the north the Chaldeans seized the valley of the Araxes River and went as far as the Great Caucasian Mountain Range. During their successful campaigns against their neighbors, the Chaldeans destroyed settlements and forts, carried off rich spoils and herds, and either slew the inhabitants or captured and made them slaves. King Argishti, in an inscription engraved on a cliff at Van, records the massacre and enslaving of over 64,000 people effected by him in a single campaign. Thousands of slaves dug canals, were employed in economy, and built impregnable castles on high cliffs on the domains belonging to the king of Urartu and his lords. The buildings were erected without the use of mortar, merely by pressing stones tightly against each other. Spacious dwellings were also hewn out of stone cliffs. This demanded a tremendous expenditure of labor. The intricate water supply and irrigation systems were amazing engineering feats. The canal which supplied drinking water to the capital, Van, remained in use for over two thousand years.

Grain and grape vines were cultivated in the irrigated regions and river valleys. Livestock breeding was of great economic importance. The Chaldeans were noted for their excellent bronze weapons and other bronze articles. Urartu was a state of slaveowners, the population being divided into freemen and slaves. The richest slaveowners were the king and his chief courtiers.

At the end of the 8th century B.C. the power of Urartu began noticeably to wane. Nomads from the north pressed the Chaldeans hard. The Assyrian empire on the Tigris grew strong again. Sargon, the Assyrian king, routed the troops of the Urartu ruler, destroyed his capital, and carried off tremendous booty. Sargon carved the following inscription on a cliff as a record of his victory: "When the king of Urartu learned of the defeat of his troops, his heart quivered with fear, as the heart of a bird fleeing from an eagle."

In the middle of the 6th century B.C. the Persian kingdom lying southeast of Urartu grew in power. The Chaldean tribes were weakened by their struggle against it. Their union under the rule of the Urartu kings had begun to disintegrate. The very name, Chaldean, fell into disuse; Urartu was retained in the name Mt. Ararat.

New tribal unions were formed on the former territory of Urartu in the 6th Century B.C., which later developed into two

11

nations— the Georgians and Armenians. The ancient Armenians lived on the land around Lake Van. The Karthveli (Karthli) and other kindred tribes who lived in the valleys of the Araxes and Kura rivers and the adjacent mountainous regions formed the Georgian people. At the end of the 6th century B.C. Armenia was compelled to submit to the rule of the Persian king, Darius I Hystaspes. Darius has left a lengthy inscription about his conquests, in which he describes how the Armenians rose up in rebellion against him, and how this rebellion was crushed only after five bloody engagements. Armenia had to pay heavy tribute to the Persian king.

CHAPTER 11

ANCIENT PEOPLES OF CENTRAL ASIA

In the first millennium B.C. the vast steppes of Central Asia were inhabited by numerous nomad tribes of herdsmen. According to the Greeks, these people were noted for their warlike spirit and bravery. All their weapons—arrows, spears, swords, axes were made exclusively of copper and bronze. Women enjoyed great freedom and even took command in time of war.

In the fertile river valleys the population engaged in agriculture. Among the agricultural people the clan system had already begun to disintegrate. Husbandry was carried on by a large patriarchal family which also included the slaves. Slave labor was used for the building of artificial reservoirs and canals, which were of great importance in arid areas. The most important agricultural regions were Khoresm (Khwarizm) along the lower reaches of the Amu Darya, and Sogdiana on the Zeravshan River.

Caravan routes crossed Central Asia, connecting the Caspian countries with Eastern Asia. The towns situated along these routes plied an active trade. The largest of these towns was Marakanda (now called Samarkand), the principal city of Sogdiana.

CHAPTER 12

CAMPAIGN OF ALEXANDER THE GREAT IN CENTRAL ASIA

In the 4th century B.C. Greece and Persia contended for world supremacy. Alexander, king of Macedonia, invaded Asia Minor, Iraq and Persia. He dreamed of conquering India. He defeated the army of the last Persian king, Darius III, and in the spring of the year 329 B.C. crossed the Hindu Kush Mountains and descended the the Central Asiatic plain, attracted by its natural resources and large population.

The inhabitants of Sogdiana desperately resisted the Macedonians. Taking advantage of Alexander's absence—he had set off for Syr Darya with the bulk of his forces—the rebellious population, led by Spitamen, massacred the Macedonian garrisons in the towns. Alexander the Great hastily returned to Sogdiana and devastated the land wantonly. However, in spite of their fearful losses, the people continued to resist. Spitamen, with detachments of horsemen, made unexpected sallies against the Macedonians and kept them in a state of constant alarm. After a protracted struggle, the Macedonians succeeded in routing Spitamen, who then retired to the steppes with the nomads who had been his allies. The nomads, however, fearing the Macedonians' vengeance murdered Spitamen and sent his head to Alexander. Thus did this outstanding leader of the Sogdians meet his end. Having completed the conquest of Central Asia Alexander the Great marched against India. He died in the year 323 B.C., while he was preparing for new conquests.

Following the death of Alexander the Great his empire, which consisted of a large number of conquered lands in no way united among themselves, fell apart. Several independent states, headed by the descendants of Macedonian generals, were formed on the territory conquered by Alexander. Greek (Hellenic) culture began to penetrate into the East after its conquest by Alexander. Greek warriors paved the way for merchants and craftsmen. Commerce between the Eastern countries and Greece increased.

Greek art considerably influenced the art of the Eastern peoples. For this reason the Eastern states formed as a result of Alexander the Great's conquests are called "Hellenic."

The state of the Seleucids (named after one of Alexander's generals, Seleucus) was founded in Syria. It subjugated Transcaucasia including Georgia and Armenia, and part of Central Asia including Sogdiana. Gradually the population of these lands threw off the yoke of the Seleucid state.

In the 3rd century B.C., Bactria became an independent state. Bactria (the territory of modern Tajikistan) was a flourishing slaveowning state at that period, and at various times included separate parts of Sogdiana, Ferghana, Kazakhstan, Afghanistan and Northwestern India.

Bactria maintained intercourse with Siberia, which supplied gold to Central Asia, and with the Urals, where metal was mined. It also had ties with China, to which country a so-called "silk route" had been laid. The Bactrian kingdom reached the zenith of its development in the 2nd century B.C.

CHAPTER 13

ARMENIA UNDER TIGRANES II

After the destruction of the Seleucid state by the Romans in the year 190 B.C. the Armenians rebelled against the Syrians and formed an independent slaveowning kingdom with its own dynasty of rulers. Armenia was at its greatest during the 1st century B.C. under Tigranes II, who crushed the might of the neighboring Parthian king in Asia Minor, Persia and Turkmenia. Following this victory Tigranes II called himself the "king of kings" and even declared himself a god. He established a magnificent Eastern court at which he gave refuge to Greek philosophers and writers who had fled from Roman oppression. During his campaigns Tigranes II captured large numbers of Greeks, Jews and Arabs, and settled them in his towns. With the help of these settlers he tried to develop the crafts and trade.

Tigranes II governed the country with the help of the rich slaveowners. Slaves cultivated the lands belonging to the king, the temples and the rich nobility. Tigranes II had a large, well-organized army. If necessary he raised a popular levy of slaveowners and their people. The army was organized on the Roman system.

CHAPTER 14

GEORGIA AND ALBANIA

Georgia, which comprised two large countries—Iberia and Colchis—was situated north of Armenia. Colchis was the name of a country bordering on the eastern extremity of the Black Sea famous for its auriferous sands and silver mines. East of Colchis was Iberia. The population inhabiting its mountainous regions engaged in herding and preserved the clan system. Both agriculture and horticulture were developed in the plains. Slavery was introduced here in the 1st century B.C.

Albania was located on the western shore of the Caspian Sea. The mountainous regions and lowlands of Albania were inhabited by numerous small tribes, which were ruled by their respective petty princes. These tribes often attacked their neighbors, the Iberians (Georgians) and Armenians. Later they united under the supremacy of the strongest tribe, the Albanians. Subsequently the descendants of the people of ancient Albania were incorporated into the Azerbaijan nation.

CHAPTER 15

PEOPLES OF NORTHERN BLACK SEA REGION

The people occupying the steppeland from the Volga to the Dniester in the 8th-3rd centuries B.C. consisted of various tribes including cultivators and nomad herdsmen, who bore the common name of Scythians.

We find descriptions of the life of the Scythian nomads in the accounts of Greek writers. All the property a Scythian possessed was contained in a four-wheeled or six-wheeled nomad kibitka—a wagon with a felt tilt drawn by two or three yoke of oxen. Each kibitka was a sort of little felt home in which the women and children lived. The Scythians roamed with their herds of horses, sheep and cattle, remaining in a given spot as long as there was sufficient pasturage for their cattle. Then they would leave in search of pasture land. Among the masses of nomads was a rich ruling nobility which possessed large herds that were tended by slaves.

The Scythians were remarkable for their martial spirit and power of endurance, for their daring, and their cruelty to the enemy. They made wine-cups from the skulls of the people they killed, and quivers from their skin. A brave warrior was accorded the greatest honor. The Scythians held annual feasts at which only those who had slain one or more of the enemy were permitted to take a draught of wine from the common goblet.

Every tribe had its king who was vested with great power. When a king died, his body was placed on a cart which was drawn throughout the entire land. The inhabitants who met the body of the king had to express profound grief: they cut their hair short, cut off part of an ear, scratched their faces, pierced their left hand with arrows. Kings were buried in huge barrows. With them were laid their arms, precious gold and silver vessels, and a large number of horses. Their wives and servants were also killed and buried with them.

Scythian tombs, some of which rise to a height of 30-35 feet are extant in the south of Russia. Many of them have been excavated and a large number of interesting objects found in them are now on display in museums.

CHAPTER 16

GREEK COLONIZATION
OF THE BLACK SEA COAST

Greek slaveowners went to the Black Sea region in quests of slaves, and were also lured to that territory by its riches. They had heard that the Scythians possessed large herds of cattle and a great amount of grain, and also that there was gold in the Caucasus. Accounts of the Black Sea region have been preserved in Greek legends about the golden fleece, the adventures of Odysseus and others. The first Greeks to visit these shores were fishermen and tradesmen who bartered with the local inhabitants. Beginning with the 7th century B.C. permanent Greek colonies sprang up on the shores of the Black Sea. On the estuary of the Southern Bug and Dnieper arose the colony of Olvia; not far from modern Sevastopol was Khersones, and on the southeastern shore of the CrimeaFeodosia and Panticapaeum (now Kerch). The city of Tanais was built at the mouth of the Don by the Sea of Azov; Greek colonies also arose on the Caucasian coast.

The centre of each Greek colony was a city surrounded by a stone wall. This wall protected the Greek colonists from attack by the hostile population. Within the city wall were dwellings, stores and various public buildings, such as the temples and baths. Among these structures were some splendid works of Greek architecture, ornamented with marble columns and statues.

Trade with Greece, with Eastern lands and the peoples of Eastern Europe was of great importance for the Greek colonies on the shores of the Black Sea. Vessels sailing for Greece were loaded with grain, slaves, furs and fish, while Greece exported weapons, fabrics, various utensils of clay and glass, costly ornaments and articles of luxury, and wine. Part of these imported goods went to satisfy the needs of the upper class of the local Greek population; part was exchanged for grain and other products supplied by the population of the northern Black Sea coast. Later the Greek cities developed their own crafts. Many of the articles found in the Scythian barrows were made in the workshops of the Black Sea colonies. The free Greek population in the colonies, as in Greece itself, met at "popular assemblies" to discuss various questions and to elect their functionaries. The entire administration was in the hands of the rich slaveowners and merchants.

Every city-colony constituted a separate state. One such city, Panticapaeum ruled a considerable territory, then so-called Bosporus kingdom. It was governed both by Greek and Scythian slaveowners, whose power was passed by inheritance from father to son.

At the end of the 3rd century B.C. the condition of the Greek colonies along the Black Sea shore deteriorated. Tribes of nomads, Sarmatae, who were kin to the Scythians appeared on the Caspian steppes. Harassed by the Sarmatae, some of the Scythians, and other nomads moved westward and reached the Danube; others went to the Crimea and occupied its northern steppes.

The Scythians who remained were assimilated by the Sarmatae and other tribes. The Greek cities found increasing diffi-culty in repulsing the attacks of the nomads.

The Scythians who settled in the Crimea during the 2nd century B.C. often attacked Khersones and the Bosporus kingdom. At this time a Pontic kingdom was formed in Asia Minor, on the southern shore of the Black Sea. Khersones, which was not strong enough to defend itself, concluded a treaty with the king of Pontus, by which it was to conceive help.

CHAPTER 17

SLAVE REVOLT IN THE CRIMEA

At the end of the 2nd century B.C. the Scythian slaves in the Bosporus kingdom rose in revolt. A slave of the Bosporus king, named Saumacus, slew the king and headed the uprising. The revolt was crushed by Diophantus, a general of King Mithridates VI of Pontus, who had come to Khersones to defend it against the Scythians. He captured Saumacus and sent him to Mithridates in

Asia Minor. As a sign of their gratitude for the help rendered against the Scythians, the rulers of Khersones erected a bronze statue of Diophantus in the acropolis of the city near the alter of their most revered goddess. An inscription telling of the services and victories of Diophantus was carved on the marble pedestal. The inscription was found among the ruins of Khersones.

The uprising of the slaves in the Crimea was not an isolated instance. Similar mass rebellions of slaves occurred in the 2nd and 1st centuries B.C. in many other slaveowning states—in Asia Minor, Greece, Italy, on the Island of Sicily and other places. These rebellions portended the end of the slaveowning system.

CHAPTER 18

ROMAN CONQUESTS IN THE BLACK SEA REGION

During the 1st century B.C. Roman dominions rapidly spread eastward. In order to conquer Asia Minor Rome had to destroy the kingdoms of Pontus and Armenia. The struggle between Rome and King Mithridates VI of Pontus lasted almost 18 years. Finally, the Roman legions inflicted a serious defeat on Mithridates. Roman slaveowners invaded the domains of Tigranes II. They sacked the rich capital of Armenia (the city of Tigranocerta on the Tigris River). The people rose in defense of their land and inflicted a series of defeats upon the Romans. Other legions under Pompey were then sent against Tigranes II. Georgians, Medes and other peoples joined the Armenians against the Romans. Pompey took advantage of dissension among the Armenian nobility and forced Tigranes II to conclude peace. The Armenian king was named the "friend and ally of the Roman people," a title which signified the subordination of Armenia to Rome. Subsequently the Romans subjugated a considerable part of Georgia.

During the 1st century B.C. the Romans established themselves firmly in the Black Sea region. The kings of Bosporus became the vassals of the Roman emperors and submissively executed all their orders. Roman legions were quartered in Khersones and other Greek cities of the Crimea and the Caucasus. Roman fortresses with towers from which the approach of enemy vessels could be observed, were built along the shore of the Black Sea.

The kings of Bosporus began to use the names of Roman emperors and to wear Roman clothing. They received their insignia of royalty from Rome: the sceptre with an image of the emperor and the royal crown. Throughout the centurylong existence of the Greek colonies, the descendants of the former colonists intermingled with the local population. Alien people of various tribes made their home in the Black Sea towns and became local citizens. In the Crimea, too, there was a mingling of different peoples and cultures.

With the decline of the Roman empire, its influence in the Black Sea countries decreased still further. By the 3rd century A.D. the Roman fortresses in the Crimea and along the Caucasian shore became desolated. The former Greek cities became independent once again. A new union of tribes, known as the Goths, was formed on the southern steppes of the Black Sea region in the 3rd century. This union also included the eastern Germans, who had formerly inhabited the lower reaches of the Vistula. Towards the middle of the 3rd century the Goths began to invade Roman dominions beyond the Danube. At the same time Goth pirates plundered the Caucasian and Asia Minor coasts of the Black Sea and penetrated to the Aegean Sea, burning Greek towns. In the 4th century the Goths were severely defeated by the Romans.

The attack of the Goths upon Rome's eastern possessions marked the beginning of the struggle of various East European tribes against the Romans. During the same period a struggle was being waged in Western Europe between the Romans and the German tribes. The attacks of the "barbarians" (non-Romans) hastened the downfall of the slaveowning Roman empire.

CHAPTER 19

NOMADS OF ASIA
(3rd Century B.C. to the 8th Century A.D.)

The vast steppes of Southern Siberia and Central Asia were inhabited by various tribes of nomads that later formed the Turkic and Mongolian peoples. Several centuries before our era the nomads living north of China formed a large tribal union. The Chinese called the nomads belonging to this union Huns. The Chinese waged an arduous struggle against the Huns, which lasted for centuries. The nomads made sudden raids on China's northern territories, sacked the towns, ruined the harvest and carried off the population. When a large Chinese army was rallied, the nomads returned to the steppe and dispersed over its boundless expanses.

In order to defend their frontiers the Chinese, as far back as the 3rd century B.C., constructed solid stone fortifications which became known as the "Great Wall of China." Gradually Chinese influence made itself felt among the nomads. The Hun chief assumed the title of "born of Heavens and the earth, the chosen of the sun and the moon." The Hun princes sent their sons to serve at the court of the Chinese emperor.

The nomad ruling caste adopted Chinese customs and Chinese clothing. A Soviet expedition to Northern Mongolia, headed by P.K. Kozlov, which explored the exceedingly rich barrows of the Hun rulers, discovered chariots, Chinese silks, a magnificent rug picturing a winged animal tearing an elk apart, precious objects, parasols which were symbols of high honor, and other objects.

The great Hun state decayed in the 1st century B.C. A large number of Huns moved westward. New tribes formerly under the domination of the Huns now came to the fore in the steppes of Asia.

CHAPTER 20

INVASION OF EASTERN EUROPE
BY THE NOMADS

When the Hun state collapsed in Mongolia, some of the tribes moved westward in their attempt to escape the Chinese. Their descendants after intermingling with other peoples in the course of their roamings, appeared in Eastern Europe in the 4th century A.D. Contemporaries of the Huns called them "the fiercest warriors." Besides the Mongolian Huns, the Hun kingdom included the native population of Central Asia and the northern part of the Black Sea region.

The Huns defeated the Goths and drove them west. The main Hun horde stopped between the Danube and the Tisia. For a brief space of time there was a strong Hun state in this locality, the king of which was Attila. After his death in 453, the Hun kingdom broke up; some of the Huns settled on the right bank of the Danube and mixed with the local population; others returned to their native haunts in the Black Sea steppes, where they were ethnically assimilated by the local population. BEGINS THE COSSACK BLOODLINE.

The movement of the Huns west of the Volga along the northern shores of the Black Sea stimulated the migration of other tribes was well. Close upon the heels of the Huns, the Bulgars came to the Caspian steppes. But the Bulgars, too, were not long able to withstand the pressure of other nomads. The Bulgarian tribal union broke up into several parts. Some of these settled on the Volga (in the Bulgarian kingdom); others reached the Balkans, where they intermingled with the local Yugoslavic population, to whom it gave its ethnic name—Bulgar. Even today they fight among themselves for ethnic cleansing as in Yugoslavia.

CHAPTER 21

TURKIC KHANATE

A group of tribes, known as the Turkic khanate, arose in Mongolia in the 6th century a.d. The ruler of this state was called a kaghan. A large number of nomad and, to some extent, agricultural tribes were under the rule of this khanate. The ruling tribes under the leadership of their khan constantly raided their neighbors and spread their power over a vast territory. The rich and the nobles commanded the warrior detachments and governed the subjugated tribes. The bulk of the nomad population lived in separate clan communities.

Tombstones of Turkic khans, bearing engraved inscriptions of remarkable campaigns and outstanding events, have been preserved in the valley of the Orkhon River.

The Turkomans of the khanate were hostile to the Turkic Kirghiz (Khakass) who inhabited the upper reaches of the Yenisei River and the Altai Mountains. One of the inscriptions tells how a Turkic khan mounted his white stallion and set off with his troops against the Kirghiz. He threw one Kirghiz off his horse. Then with a spear in his hand, he rushed into the ranks of the enemy. while doing so he dug his spurs into his white horse so violently, that he broke the horse's ribs. The Kirghiz khan was killed and the people submitted to the power of the Turkic khan.

The Turkic state in Mongolia and Central Asia collapsed in the 8th century A.D. After the fall of the Turkic khanate, the Kirghiz (Khakass), who had as many as 80,000 warriors and a large population proved to be the strongest people.

And so throughout many centuries the vast lands of Southern Siberia and Central Asia saw the continuous rise and fall of one or another tribal union. The nomads in their search for better pasturage and plunder, traversed a large section of the Central Asiatic steppes. Part of the nomads settled in the new places; others continued further west. They were drawn to those regions by the fertile, grassy plains which spread out like a heavy green blanket northwest of the Caspian Sea.

CHAPTER 22

EARLY FEUDAL STATES IN TRANSCAUCASIA

THE STRUGGLE BETWEEN ROME AND PERSIA (IRAN) FOR ARMENIA AND GEORGIA

Rome ceased to exist as a slaveowning empire in the 4th-5th centuries A.D. The peoples of Europe and Asia, including those of Parthia and Persia, rose against her. Persia subjugated Parthia, Albania (Azerbaijan) and a considerable part of Georgia and Armenia. Only a small part of Western Armenia and Western Georgia remained under Roman power. At the end of the 4th century the Roman empire fell apart and was divided into two empires: the Eastern and the Western. The Eastern Roman empire (Byzantium) continued its struggle against Persia for possession of Armenia and Georgia.

CHAPTER 23

THE BIRTH OF FEUDALISM IN ARMENIA AND GEORGIA

About the middle of the 1st century A.D. the Arsacid dynasty was established in Armenia. With great solemnity the Roman Emperor, Nero, received an Armenian embassy and personally placed a crown upon the head of the Armenian king. It was approximately in the 4th century A.D., when kings of the Arsacid dynasty were in power, that feudal relations originated in Armenia. Slave labor was not very productive and even became unprofitable with the development of agriculture and the crafts and improvements in working tools. It was therefore superseded by the labor of feudal subjects. Serfs who lived on the lands of their feudal lords had their own little farms and the necessary implements. They tilled the land of the feudal lord and fulfilled other services for him.

The lord could no longer kill his serf with impunity, as he had killed the slave, but he still retained the right to buy and sell serfs.

Under serfdom the peasant was interested, to a certain degree, in husbandry as a means of livelihood and to pay his lord a tax in kind, that is, with the products of his own harvest. The big landowners forced the peasants to do all the work on their estates and to render all manner of service. Every rich feudal lord had his own castle and troops. The feudal nobility seized the most important posts. The great feudal lords formed the king's court, and attended state ceremonies at which they occupied places according to seniority.

At the end of the 3rd century A.D. the Armenian king and nobility adopted Christianity from Byzantium, and it became the national religion of Armenia. Byzantium supported the Christian church, using it to strengthen her influence. The church contributed to the final establishment of feudalism in Armenia, though ancient pagan beliefs persisted for a long time among the peasant population.

In the Byzantine part of Armenia the power of the king was destroyed at the end of the 4th century, and the country was ruled by Byzantine officials appointed by the emperor. Similarly the rule of the king in that part of Armenia which was under Persian sway soon came to an end. With the termination of the king's rule the power of the large landowners was still further augmented.

Mesrob Mashtots, a monk, born of a peasant family, perfected the Armenian alphabet in the early part of the 5th century. This marked the beginning of an Armenian literature; instruction in the schools was carried on in the native language; youths were sent to Egypt and Byzantium to perfect their knowledge of the sciences. An extensive literature, both original and translated, appeared.

A kingdom was formed in Western Georgia on the territory of ancient Colchis in the 4th century A.D. This land was inhabited by ancient Georgian tribes of Lazis, whence the Romans and Greeks derived their name for the land (Lazica). The center of this land was the fertile valley of Rion, which was covered with vineyards and orchards. This valley was also the site of a considerable number of towns, including Kutaisi, which engaged in commerce. After a long struggle with Persia, Lazica remained under Byzantine rule. The Eastern Georgian lands formed part of another kingdom, Karthli (ancient Iberia). In the beginning of the 5th century the king of Karthli became a vassal of Persia. As everywhere else, the development of feudal relations in Georgia enhanced the power of the landowning nobility, which tried to limit the king's power. Christianity began to penetrate into Georgia via the cities along the Black Sea shore. With the aid of Byzantium it became firmly established as the state religion of Karthli in the middle of the 4th century, and in Lazica in the beginning of the 6th century. Christianity strengthened the cultural ties between Georgia and Byzantium. Translations of religious writings appeared simultaneously with translations of Greek philosophical and historical works. This stimulated the growth of Georgian literature. The peoples of Transcaucasia did not cease their struggle for liberation. At the end of the 5th century the Karthlian king, Vakhtang, who was called the "Wolf's Head" because of the emblem in the form of a wolf's head on his helmet, fought against Persia. During one of the engagements he was mortally wounded. After his death the Persian feudal lords assumed power. The country was then ruled by a Persian satrap who settled in Tbilisi.

CHAPTER 24

THE STRUGGLE OF THE PEOPLES OF TRANSCAUCASIA AGAINST PERSIAN AND BYZANTINE DOMINATION

Byzantine and Persian domination in Georgia, Armenia and Albania (Azerbaijan) was accompanied by the terrible oppression and devastation of these lands. The population was brought to the point of despair by intolerable tribute and compulsory services. The conquerors conscripted the Armenian and Georgian youth into their armies. These conditions led to frequent bloody popular uprisings in Georgia, Armenia and Albania (Azerbaijan). The rebellions were notably powerful when the Georgians and Armenians joined forces against the common enemy. Filled with hatred for the enslavers, these peoples won many a victory over numerous and better armed enemy detachments. While the people fought heroically and staunchly for the liberation of their country, the rich feudal lords often turned traitors and went over to the camp of their country's enemies. This made it easier for Persia and Byzantium to crush the uprisings of the people.

CHAPTER 25

STRUGGLE OF THE PEOPLES OF TRANSCAUCASIA AGAINST THE ARABS

Persia's rule in Armenia and Georgia lasted until the 7th century, when the Arabs, soon after reducing the Persian empire, conquered Transcaucasia and Central Asia. In 642 they seized the capital of Armenia, Dvin, and within a few years conquered all of Armenia and Eastern Georgia. In the 9th-10th centuries there was a considerable number of rich cities in Transcaucasia—Tbilisi (Tiflis), Derbent, and others, which carried on trade and the crafts and maintained intercourse with Eastern Europe. Tbilisi became the residence of the Arabian emir. The country was ruled by his ostikans (governors). With the arrival of the Arabs, the Moslem faith spread among the people of Transcaucasia.

The peasants of Transcaucasia frequently rose in revolt against their Arabian Conquerors, who were ruining the land with their exactions and turning the local population into slaves and serfs. A big uprising of peasants, craftsmen and slaves occurred in the first half of the 9th century in Azerbaijan, under the leadership of the gallant chieftain Babek. Babek was orphaned when still a child. After his father's death, when he was only 10 years old, the boy was turned over to a rich herdsman, for whom he worked as shepherd. Later he became a camel driver. This enabled him to study the life of the Azerbaijan people at first hand. The sufferings of these people, oppressed by heavy taxes and other exactions, aroused in Babbek a feeling of irrecon cilable hatred for the oppressors and enslavers, especially for the Arabian rule. Babek, who was only 18 years old at that time, joined a popular uprising and soon became it's leader. Finding protection in the inaccessible, high mountain regions, Babek fought tenaciously against the Arabs. The rebels won several victories over powerful Arabian detachments.

It was only after long years of struggle that the Arabs succeeded in occupying the chief insurgent areas. Babek went into hiding in the mountains and from there he continued guerilla warfare against the Arabs and the local feudal lords who had betrayed their own people. All attempts to surround and capture Babek failed. Then one of the powerful feudal lords, pretending to be a supporter of Babek's, turned him over to the Arabs. He was executed upon the order of the caliph. The uprising was suppressed. This determined struggle of the Azerbaijan people for independence lasted over twenty years.

The disintegration of the Arab caliphate, which began at the end of the 9th century, led to the restoration of the rule of the local wealthy families in Georgia and Armenia.

In 864 Ashod I, who represented one of the most powerful families of Armenia, became king of Armenia and founded a new dynasty of the Bagratids, which ruled until the middle of the 11th century. This dynasty succeeded in uniting a large part of Armenia. The city of Ani (not far from the city of Kars) became the capital of the Bagratids and the trade center between the East and the West. The city was beautified by a number of splendid buildings which point to the flourishing state of Armenian architecture.

After the fall of the Arab caliphate, Georgia broke up into a number of rival independent feudal principalities. It was only in the second half of the 10th century that one of these, the Tao-Klarzhetsk, succeeded in uniting these principalities under the power of the kings of the Georgian Bagratid dynasty.

CHAPTER 26

ARMENIAN EPIC
"DAVID OF SASUN"

The memory of the age-long struggle of the Armenian people against their conquerors, the Arabs, has come down to us in a beautiful poem, David of Sasun. It tells of the adventures and feats of four generations of Armenian knights. Two brothers built a fortress of huge stones high in the mountains which they named Sasun ("Wrath"). Poor people came to Sasun from all parts of the country to seek protection, and it became the bulwark of the people's struggle against the enemies of their native land.

CHAPTER 27

PEOPLES OF CENTRAL ASIA IN THE STRUGGLE AGAINST THE ARABS

CONQUEST OF CENTRAL ASIA BY THE ARABS

At the time of the Arabian conquest, Central Asia consisted of several states which were constantly at war with each other. The most important of these was Sogdiana, a land of fertile oasis, rich foothills and mountain valleys. It's territory was studded with the castles of landowning princelings who were practically independent of each other. The Most powerful of them was the ruler of Samarkand, who called himself the "Sogdianan king." West of Samarkand was Bodhara. Along the lower reaches of the Amu Darya stood Khoresm.

The steppes of Central Asia were populated by nomad tribes. The incursions of Turkic tribes from the east grew more insistent. In the early part of the 8th century they tried to seize the agricultural regions of Central Asia and it's rich commercial cites, but were repulsed by the Arabs.

In 751, Arabs routed both the Turkomans and the Chinese on the banks of the Talass River and also conquered Central Asia.

The population of Sogdiana—the Sogdians, remote ancestors of the Tajiks—desperately resisted the Arab aggression. This agricultural people found an ally in the nomads, who came to their aid. It took the Arabs about 75 years to completely subjugate the lands between the Amu Darya and Syr Darya. Khoresm, Sogdiana, Bokhara and other Central Asiatic lands became part of the Arab caliphate in the middle of the 8th century. In most cases the Arabs permitted the local princelings to retain their lands and power, but made them their tributaries. The caliph sent his governors to the larger cities and established permanent Arabian garrisons there.

The prosperous merchants took advantage of the Arabian conquest to trade with the caliphate dominions. Large numbers of Arabs settled in the towns, and noticeably influenced the local culture. The Moslem faith spread among the ruling class of the local population, and the Arabian tongue became the language of literature and of the state.

The agricultural population, who had heretofore rendered various services to their landowners, now also had to pay heavy taxes in kind to the Arabs. This tax sometimes amounted to as much as half their crops. The people, the peasants, slaves and indigent city population, were in constant rebellion against the Arab yoke.

CHAPTER 28

THE REVOLT OF MOKANNA

The greatest uprising took place in the seventies of the 8th century. It was called the revolt of "the white-shirted", since the peasants wore simple white clothing. The leader of the popular rebellion was Hashim-ibn Hakim, who was known among the people as Mokanna, which means "The Veiled".

Mokanna used to wash clothes in his youth. Later he had command of one of the rebel detachments. He was captured by the

Arabs and spent some years in a dungeon, but succeeded in escaping, and began to prepare a general uprising of the peasants against the Arabs and local landowners. This rebellion lasted about seven years. The insurgents seized and destroyed castles, killed the local landowners who had joined the enemies of their native land, and wiped out the Arabian garrisons in the towns. To subdue the peasant uprising, the Arabian emirs raised a huge army equipped with battering rams. Several fierce battles took place in which the peasant army suffered heavy defeats. Mokanna was killed, but the people did not cease to rebel against the Arabs.

CHAPTER 29

THE STATE OF THE SAMANIDS

When the Arab caliphate collapsed in Central Asia in the second half of the 9th century, the ancient Tajik state of the Samanids was formed (subsequently the name Tajik was given to the native Sogdiana population), with the city of Bokhara as it's capital. The kings of the Samanid dynasty tried to create a strong, centralized power, such as was necessary to combat the nomads. They stubbornly opposed individual petty rulers who tried to establish an independent rule.

Thanks to the power of the Samanids, quiet set in in the Central Asiatic steppes. This stimulated trade and life in the cities. The largest cities (Bokhara, Samarkand and Merv) engaged in a lively trade with eastern and western countries, particularly with China and the Volga region.

Literature and learning flourished during the reign of the Samanids. Poets and scholars (philosophers, doctors, geographers, mathematicians, historians and others) created an exceedingly rich literature in the Arabian and Persian languages. Numerous valuable manuscripts were stored in the royal library at Bokhara. Each department of science or literature in the library had a special room to itself, and the library had an efficiently-kept catalogue. the famous philosopher, naturalist and doctor, Avicenna (ibn-Sina) lived and worked in Bokhara at the end of the 10th century. Later his works were translated into Latin and became widespread in medieval Europe.

CHAPTER 30

KHAZARS AND BULGARS ON THE VOLGA

The Turkic-Khazars formed a strong Khazar state on the Lower Volga in the 7th century. The Khazars were a semi-nomad people. In the winter they lived in the cities, and in the spring they took their herds out to the steppes to graze. Herding remained their chief occupation, although they also engaged in agriculture, and grapevine cultivation. The Khazars were still divided into clans, each of which possessed it's own section ofland. However, the clan system had already begun to decay, and an influential group of the nobility in the clan came to the fore. The Khazar kingdom was headed by a khakan or king, who was surrounded by rich dignitaries. The king was rendered divine homage. The country, however, was governed by a lord lieutenant and not by the Khakan himself.

The Khakan lived in Itil, a populous city situated upon the delta of the Volga. Outside the city walls were wooden dwellings and felt nomad tents. The royal brick palace was situated on an island connected with the bank by a floating bridge. The eastern side of the city was inhabited by visiting merchants—people from Khoresm, Arabs, Greeks, Jews and others. The many markets here had a diversity of wares from Central Asia, the Caucasus, the Volga region and the Slavonic lands. Itil was an important center for southeastern trade, and it's commercial intercourse with Khoresm as of especial importance. The duty which the merchants paid the Khazars constituted one of the chief sources of income for the khakan's treasury. The regular intercourse with Transcaucasia and Khoresm had an important influence on the constitution of the Khazar state and the everyday life of it's population. The Khazar ruling class and the king embraced Judaism.

Another important Khazar city was Sarkel on theDon. Sarkel was built with the help of Byzantine engineers, and was intended to afford protection against irruptions of nomads form the north and the east.

The Khazar state reached the zenith of it's power in the 9th century. In the south the Khazars in alliance with Byzantium fought against the Arabs and even went as far as the Araxes River. West of the Volga, the lands between the Caspian and Azov seas belonged to the Khazars, who at one time had subjugated part of the Crimea and imposed tribute upon the Slavonic tribes living along the Dnieper and the Oka rivers. In the north their power extended to the middle reaches of the Volga.

The closest neighbors of the Khazars were the Pechenegs, who in the 9th century, roamed between the Yaik (the Ural) River and the Volga. Harassed by other nomad tribes as well as by the Khazars, the Pechenegs moved further west in the second half of the 9th century, and occupied the steppe between the Don and the Dnieper.

CHAPTER 31

BULGAR STATE ON THE VOLGA AND KAMA

The union of Bulgar tribes on the Volga broke up as a result of the constant attacks of other nomads. Some of the Bulgars migrated to the Danube. Here they were absorbed by the Slavs, but they handed down their own tribal name to these people. Others went north up the Volga and settled on the lands along the lower reaches of the Kama and the Middle Volga, where they formed an independent state. During this period of migration to the Kama and the Volga, the Bulgars were still nomads. In their new environment they turned to agriculture. According to the accounts of Arab writers, the Bulgars cultivated wheat, barley and millet.

In the Bulgar state the power belonged to the king, the tribal chieftains and the tribal nobility. Most of the towns were situated near the confluence of the Kama and the Volga. The Arabs called the Bulgar capital on the Volga, the "Great City". Merchants from the Slav lands, from Transcaucasia, Byzantium and Central

Asia, paid annual visits to the capital of Bulgaria. From the Slav lands they brought strong, stalwart slaves and valuable furs. Arabian merchants came with steel swords, silk and cotton fabrics, and various rich ornaments.

The Bulgars themselves made journeys for furs to the north, which they called the "land of Gloom". They bartered with the trappers of that country. The Bulgar merchants would lay out their wares in a pre-arranged spot and then depart. The following day they would find animal skins set out beside their own goods. If the Bulgar merchant was satisfied with the bargain, he took the furs and left his own wares. If not, he would not touch the skins but would take back his own goods. Arabian culture, which was more highly developed, penetrated Bulgaria with the eastern trade. By the 10th century the ruling class of Bulgars had already taken over the Moslem faith from the Arabs. In imitation of the Arabs, the Bulgars began to mint their own coins.

In the beginning of the 10th century, ibn-Fadhlan visited Bulgaria as a member of an Arabian embassy. He left a most interesting description of his travels. The Bulgar king met the embassy not far from the capital. The envoys were ushered into a large, richly appointed tent, with Armenian rugs spread on the ground. The king sat on a throne covered with Byzantine brocades. On his right hand sat the chiefs of his subject tribes. During the feast the guests were regaled with chunks of meat and drinks made of honey. Ibn-Fadhlan also saw Russian merchants there. They were strong stalwart people. Each of them was armed with a battle-ax, a knife and a sword, with which he never parted.

After the formation of the Bulgar and Khazar kingdoms, the Volga became a very important trade route between Europe and Asia. It's upper reaches closely approach the Western Dvina, which flows into the Baltic Sea. Thus, there was an almost complete river route between the Caspian and the Baltic seas. Where there was a break in the river system, boats were hauled overland by "portage".

Arabian merchants came in great numbers to trade on the Volga in the 8th-10th centuries. They paid for their purchases with dirhems, small silver Arabian coins, which were current throughout Eastern Europe, including the Baltic states, Scandinavia and even Germany.

CHAPTER 32

FORMATION OF KIEV STATE

THE SLAVS IN THE 6TH-7TH CENTURIES

The ancestors of the Slavs, one of the most numerous peoples in Europe, inhabited the greater part of Eastern Europe since time immemorial. According to Roman writers of the 1st and 2nd centuries A.D., who knew the Slavs as Venedi, the Slavs lived along the Vistula and on the southern shore of the Baltic Sea.

Byzantine writers of the 6th century referred to the Eastern Slavs as Antes. The Eastern Slavs lived in the region of the Carpathians, the lower reaches of the Danube, along the Kniester, the Knieper and the Don, occupying almost the whole of the southern part of Eastern Europe as far as the coasts of the Black Sea and Azov Sea. The Eastern Slavs engaged in agriculture, herding, fishing and hunting. They were also acquainted with the working of metals. Their dwellings consisted of huts made of interwoven brushwood or reeds covered with clay. Their villages were surrounded by ditches, earthen ramparts, and wooden walls.

The Eastern Slavs at that time still preserved the clan system. All matters of tribal concern were decided at tribal meetings called the veche (from the word veshchat meaning to speak). Influential members of the community became head-men or princes; some of them were influential not only in their own, but in neighboring tribes as well.

Patriarchal slavery existed amoung the Eastern Slavs, but slave labor did not play a significant role in their economy. Captives were either sold to foreign merchants, were permitted to return to their own land for ransom, or, after spending several years in captivity, were given their freedom and the right to stay in the community as freemen.

Beginning with the 5th century, the Eastern and Western Slavs, year after year, ravaged the Danube lands which formed part of the Byzantine empire. Tall, strong and very hardy, the Slavs were inured to heat, cold and hunger. In war they displayed great adroitness and cunning, and though armed only with shields and javelins, rushed boldly at the enemy. During the wars with Byzantium the Slavs mastered the Byzantine military art and acquired weapons which they learned to use even better than the Byzantines themselves.

From the 6th century the Slavs no longer confined themselves to raiding the frontier regions of the Byzantine empire, but also began to settle on the conquered lands. They peopled the entire northern part of the Balkan Peninsula almost as far as Constantinople and even penetrated the Peloponnesus.

A nomad horde of Bulgars invaded the Danube Valley in the 7th century. Culturally, the Danube Slavs, an agricultural people, were far superior to the Bulgar herdsmen. This explains why the Bulgars who settled on the Danube lands were quickly Slavonicized. The descendants of the Bulgar princes headed the Slavonic kingdom which was formed at the end of the 7th century south of the Danube and which was called Bulgaria (or Bulgaria on the Danube, in contradistinction to Bulgaria on the Kama).

CHAPTER 33

SALVONIC TRIBES IN THE 8TH-9TH CENTURIES

In the 8th and 9th centuries the Eastern Slavs split up into several tribes. The Slavonic tribes which had once inhabited the Black Sea steppes and it's shores had, for the most part, been swept away by the influx of nomads. The Polyane (from the word polye meaning field) lived along the middle reaches of the Dnieper in the region of kiev, bordering on the steppe. The land west of the Polyane (in the western regions of the present Ukraine) was inhabited by the Dulebi or Volynyane (Volhynians), while south of them, in what today is Moldavia as far as the Lower Danube dwelt the Tivertsi and Ulichi. Northwest of the Polyane, as far as the Pripyat, a tributary of the Knieper, were the Drevlyane, the "forest dwellers".

One of the beliefs of the Slavs was that the souls of the dead continued to live after death. Food was left on the graves for the deceased. Their funeral rites were in conformity with the cult of the dead. Not all Slav tribes had the same rites: in some places the body was buried in a grave,in others the corpse was burnt and the ashes interred. a mount was put up over the grave. The deceased was fully equipped for his future life; various household objects (a knife, flint, weapons, utensils, etc.) were laid in the grave. When a rich man died, his wife and slaves were all interred with him. A wake was held to honor the dead, attended by military games and feasting in which the dead man was supposed to be a participant.

The Eastern Slavs had no temples. Wooden idols were set up in open-air shrines. Sacrifices were made to propitiate the gods and receive their support or appease their wrath. Sometimes these were human sacrifices. The Slavs believed that there were people who could divine the will of the gods, and they called such people volkhvy, or wizards. The latter were supposed to know special incantations by which they could control the powers of nature, cure the sick, transform themselves into werewolves, etc. The pagan beliefs of the Slavs such as the belief in household gods, wood-goblins and other superstitions persisted among the people for many centuries.

CHAPTER 34

THE NEIGHBORS OF THE SLAVS

The southeastern part of the Baltic seacoast from the Niemen River to the Western Dvina was occupied by Lithuanian tribes. Those living between the Niemen and the Vistula were called Litovtsi-Prussi. The right tributaries of the Lower Niemen were inhabited by the Litovtsi-Zhmud. The region of the middle reaches of the Niemen was occupied by the Lithuanians proper (Litva). This name was later applied to all Lithuanian tribes. The right bank of the lower reaches of the Western Dvina was the home of the Letygols, and the left bank—the Zimigols (Semigallia), These two tribes subsequently formed the latvian people. The land along the watersheds flowing into the Baltic Sea was covered with dense forests and swamps. The Lithuanians lived in these forest jungles in small settlements; they had neither towns nor fortifications. Their small clan and tribal unions were in no way connected with each other. The population engaged in hunting, agriculture, and, to some extent, in herding. The Lithuanians who lived along the seacoast fished, collected amber, which was highly prized at that time, and traded with neighboring peoples (notably the Scandinavians).

Various Ural-Altaic tribes lived northeast of the Lithuanians and Slavs: the Chudes (Esths), Merya, Mordvinians, Cheremissi (Mari) and others. They occupied the forest land in the northeast of Europe. Their chief occupations were hunting and fishing. The northern woods abounded in sable, marten, squirrel, fox and other valuable fur-bearing animals. The pelts of these animals were bought by eastern merchants on the Volga and by European merchants on the shore of the Baltic. The people lived in mud-huts, selecting as sites for their settlements places which offered a natural protection and shielded them against attacks of the enemy.

CHAPTER 35

THE VARANGIANS IN EASTERN EUROPE

A water route connecting the Baltic Sea with the Black Sea ran across the land occupied by the Eastern Slavs and was called the "route from the Varangians to the Greeks", that is, from

Scandinavia, the land of the Varangians, to Byzantium. This route ran from the Gulf of Finland via the Neva River to Lake Ladoga, thence up the Volkhov River to Lake Ilmen and from Lake Ilmen to the Loval River, from which vellels were carried by portage to the upper reaches of the Western Dvina. Bands of Varangians, as the inhabitants of Scandinavia were known in Eastern Europe or Norsemen, as they were called by their southern neighbors, used this route in the 9th century when they went in quest of plunder. At that time the Norsemen terrified all Western Europe with their raids. They invaded the lands of the Eastern Slavs, as everywhere else, for predatory trade and plunder. The varangians were organized in military bands under the leadership of their konungs, or princes. They attacked the Slavs and other tribes, robbed them of their furs, took prisoners, and carried off their booty to be sold in Constantinople, or to be shipped down the Volga to the land of the Bulgars and to the khazar capital Itil. The slavs and their nieghbors repeatedly rose against these freebooters and drove them off.

Some of the Varangian princes and their retinues seized the most advantageous places on the "route from the Varangians to the Greeks" and imposed tribute upon the local Slav population. They very often killed or subordinated the local Slavonic princes and ruled in their stead. Legend has it that in the middle of the 9th century one such adventurer, Rurik, established himself in Novgorod, which was the key position to the Knieper route from the north. His brother Sineus lived at Byelo Ozero (White Lake), across which lay a route from the Gulf of Finland to the Volga and the Urals, and another brother, Truvor, at Izborsk, a town which commanded the routes to the Baltic shore. Two other Varangian chiefs Askild and Dir, took possession of the city of Kiev in the land of the Polyane. Kiev was an important southern point on the "route from the Varangians to the Greeks". Another offshoot of Scandinavia seized the principality of Polotsk on a different route leading from the Baltic Sea to the Dnieper along the Western Dvina. Most of the Varangians who made raids on Slav lands returned home with their booty. Some of the Scandinavian princes, however, settled with their retinues in the towns of Rus, sometimes entering the service of the local Slav princes to protect them from new freebooters coming from Scandinavia.

The number of Varangians who settled on Slav lands was negligible. The Varangian bands were augmented by local Slav warriors. Before long the Varangians were Slavonicized; already in the beginning of the 10th century they used the Slavonic language and worshipped Slavonic gods. The Varangian warriors very quickly merged with the Slav nobility and formed with it a single class. The ancient state of Rus grew in its struggle with the Varangians in the north and with the nomads who invaded the Black Sea steppes from the east, and maintained it's independence of Byzantium.

CHAPTER 36

UNION OF EASTERN SLAVS AROUND KIEV

THE KIEV STATE

The Dnieper region and the adjacent lands were united under the rule of Prince Oleg in the beginning of the 10th century. The chroniclers tell us that at first Oleg ruled over the Novgorod Slavs, but later went down the Knieper and conquered the Smolensk Krivichi. Proceeding further down the Dnieper, he slew Askold and Dir, who were in Kiev, took possession of the city, and reduced the neighboring Drevlyane. Oleg also subdued the tribes of Severyane and Radimichi, who had been under the Khazar yoke. The simultaneous possession of Novgorod and Kiev made Oleg the undisputed lord of the Dnieper route. The lesser princes were forced to submit to him. He became the "Grand Prince of Rus", with all other princes "under his will". The lands of the Dnieper and the Ilmen Slavs were united under the rule of the Kiev prince. This union was called Rus, and it's center was Kiev, which is why we call this union of ancient Russian lands "Kiev Rus."

The greater part of the population subject to the Kiev princes were Slavs, but their state also included the Merya, Vesi, Chudes and other tribes. The economic ties among all these tribes were weak, and the latter were therefore unable to form a stable entity.

During this period the Eastern Slavs still lived in agricultural communities (vervs) and retained various customs that had prevailed under the clan system. But the process of disintegration was already in progress in the community; individual members accumulated wealth; the labor of the poorer tribesmen was exploited. In this way the division of society into classes was hastened, private ownership of land developed, and feudal relations originated.

CHAPTER 37

CAMPAIGNS AGAINST BYZANTIUM AND THE CASPIAN COUNTRIES

The Kiev state, which consisted of a number of independent principalities loosely held together maintained itself by force of arms.

The Kiev state played an important role in Eastern Europe. In 860, as a reprisal against Byzantine aggression a large fleet of Slav odnoderevki (small craft hewn out of solid oak trunks) made it's way to the Golden Horn (the inlet of the Bosporus forming the harbor of Constantinople) and threatened the walls of Constantinople. the city was saved only because a storm dispersed the Slav fleet. The annals state that Oleg undertook a successful campaign against Constantinople. In 911, he concluded an advantageous peace with Byzantium, which established the exact relations between the Rus and the Greeks. The treaty is evidence of the regular relations between Rus and Byzantium and of the great power of the prince of Kiev.

In 913 or 914 Rus attacked the Caspian coastline. Russian vessels sailed from the Sea of Azov up the Don to the spot where this river most closely approaches the Volga, and from there, by portage, their boats were carried to the Volga. The Rus then went down to the Caspian Sea and ravaged the Transcaucasian coast (now Azerbaijan), but on the way back they themselves were attacked by the Khazars and sustained certain losses.

Oleg was succeeded in the second quarter of the 10th century by the Kiev Prince Igor, whom the annals call the son of Rurik, and who occupied a similar dominating position in relation to the other princes. Igor continued the conquests of Oleg. He subjugated the Slavs living on the Southern Bug and imposed tribute upon the Drevlyane who revolted against the rule of Kiev. In 941 Igor launched a big sea campaign against Byzantium. The Rus devastated the precincts of Constantinople, but the Greek fleet kept them out of the harbor and forced them back to the Black Sea. Repulsed from Constantinople, the Rus ravaged the northern shore of Asia Minor. The Greek government had to send a large land force to drive the Rus out of that country. The Greek fleet, which was equipped with devices for pouring liquid combustibles ("Greek fire") over enemy vessels, inflicted a telling defeat on Igor's sea force. The Greeks succeeded in setting fire to the Russian vessels. To save themselves from the "Greek fire" many of the Rus plunged into the water and were drowned. Nevertheless, what remained of the Slavonic fleet made its way past the enemy vessels and returned to its native land.

To avoid a repetition of raids by the Rus the Greeks concluded a new treaty with Igor in 945. In this treaty the trade conditions between Rus and Constantinople were set forth in detail, and a military alliance against their common enemies was established.

In 943 Rus once more undertook a big expedition against the settlements along the Caspian seacoast. Rus warriors sailed up the Kura River and captured the city of Berdaa. From there the Rus made attacks on the outlying lands. The unfavorable climatic conditions told on the Rus, of whom disease and mortality took heavy toll. Their thinned ranks were besieged in a fortress by Arab troops; however, the remnants, under cover of night, succeeded in making their way to their vessels and to return to Rus with their plunder.

CHAPTER 38

POLYUDYE

One of the reasons that prompted the Kiev state in the 10th century was that big land tenure was in the process of formation. The princes therefore exploited the population chiefly by collecting tribute from the people. The princes had bodies of military retainers (retinues) with whose help they undertook their campaigns and kept the conquered peoples in subjection. They shared the tribute they extorted with their retinue, thus paying the latter for their services. Each year, at the beginning of winter, the prince and his retinue of warriors would leave their city na polyudye, that is, on an expedition "among the people" to levy tribute. The prince would make the round of his subject domains and collect furs, honey, bees-wax, etc., from the inhabitants . In the spring the booty together with prisoners captured in war would be loaded on ships and sent down the Dnieper to the Black Sea. At the Dnieper rapids the merchandise and vessels would be transferred by portage. Here the travelers would often be beset by the Pechenegs, lying in wait to rob them of their wares. Another dangerous spot was near the island of Khortitsa (where Dnieproges, the Dnieper Power Station, now stands). The high bluffs here cramped the narrow current of the Dnieper, and a fleet of ships was always in danger of attack by the nomads.

After leaving the mouth of the Dnieper and sailing into the Black Sea, the voyages offered thanksgiving sacrifices at a "sacred" oak on a little islet. Then they followed the western shore of the Black Sea. The final destination was Constantinople, or Tsargrad (the tsar's city) as the Slavs called it. There they sold the furs, bees-wax and slaves, and in exchange acquired costly fabrics, wines, fruit and other luxuries.

Tribute was wrung from the subject tribes by violent and oppressive means, with the result that the Drevlyane, headed by their local Prince Mal, rebelled during the rule of Igor. Igor, the chronicler says, entrusted the levying of tribute from certain Slav tribes to one of his more influential retainers named Sveneld, thus arousing dissatisfaction among his guard. The latter persistently urged Igor to go to the land of the Drevlyane himself to collect tribute, saying "Sveneld's warriors have fitted themselves out with arms, clothes and horses, while we are naked. Let us go, Prince, and collect the tribute, and thou wilt gain and we will". After collecting tribute from the land of the Drevlyane, Igor dismissed most of his military retinue and decided to make another round himself. "I will return and go about some more". When the Drevlyane heard that the prince was preparing to come back for more tribute, they said "If the wolf gets into the habit of visiting a herd he will devour it all unless he is killed". They slew Igor's attendants, then captured and killed Igor himself (945).

Igor's widow, Olga (945-957), who ruled instead of her son Svyatoslav, who was in his minority, mercilessly crushed the mutiny. Iskorosten, the principal city of the Drevlyane, was taken and burned; many of the inhabitants were either slain or reduced to slavery; the rest had to pay a heavy tribute. Fearing further uprisings, Olga fixed the exact amount of tribute to be paid in the future. However, not content merely with tribute she began seizing portions of the land that still belonged to the communities. This testifies to the still greater exploitation of the conquered lands by the princes and their retainers.

CHAPTER 39

THE CONQUESTS OF SVYATOSLAV

Svyatoslav (957-972), the son of Igor and Olga, was a Slav by birth, name and appearance. He wore a simple white shirt, an earring in one of his ears, and shaved his head, leaving only a long forelock. A brave leader of a martial retinue, he spent his whole life on campaigns, "walking lightly, like a panther"; he never took any baggage carts on his marches, slept on the ground with his saddle as pillow, and ate half-cooked horseflesh. Svyatoslav never attacked an enemy by underhand, treacherous means. When setting out on a campaign he sent messengers ahead to say "I want to march against you".

The adjacent lands of the Dnieper and Lake Ilmen were already part of the Kiev state. Svyatoslav directed his arms first against the Slavonic tribes living east of the Dnieper, conquered the Vyatichi on the Oka, and then attacked the other peoples. In the sixties of the 10th century he defeated the Volga states of the Bulgars and the Khazars, then marched to the Northern Caucasus, where he defeated the Kasogi (Circassians) and Yasi (the Ossetians), In 967 Svyatoslav launched a campaign against Bulgaria on the Danube, a land inhabited by Slavs who had assumed the name of the Bulgars, their conquerors. The Bulgars were constantly attacking their neighbor, the Greek empire, inflicting serious defeats on the Greeks. Not equal to coping with Bulgar incursions the Greeks appealed to Svyatoslav for aid. He not only won a complete victory over the Bulgars, but even planned to establish himself permanently in Pereyaslavets on the Danube, the capital of Bulgaria. "Here," he said, "is the center of my land; here flows everything that is good; gold, rich fabrics, wine and fruit from the Greeks; silver and horses from Czechia and Hungary; furs, bees-wax, honey and slaves from Rus".

The Greek government, fearing such a dangerous neighbor, bribed the Pechenegs to attack Kiev. News of the siege of Kiev by the Pechenegs forced Svyatoslav to hasten back to the Knieper region. But he did not relinquish the idea of conquering Bulgaria. After driving the Pechenegs back to the steppes, he returned and recaptured Pereyaslavets. Thereupon the new Byzantine Emperor, John Tzimisces, advanced against him with a big army. Faced by a superior enemy, Svyatoslav nevertheless did not abandon the struggle. He is attributed by the chronicles to have made the following address to his warriors: "Let us not shame the Russian soil, but lay down our lives, for the dead know no shame, but if we flee, then shall we be shamed".

The Greek troops took Pereyaslavets, but not until after a hard struggle. The Rus garrison which had been left in the city by Svyatoslav barricaded itself in the royal palace of the Bulgars and defended itself even after the city fell to the enemy. Tzimisces ordered the palace to be set on fire; only then did the Rus leave the city for the field, where they fought their last battle. "They fought vigorously", writes a Greek historian; "they did not take to flight, and our men put them all to the sword". Svyatoslav shut himself up in the town of Dorostol on the Danube. He was besieged on land by Tzimisces' army, while on the Danube his retreat was blocked by the Greek fleet with it's fire-throwers. In spite of this, Svyatoslav rejected all peace offers. His army, which was very small, defended itself heroically and made daring sallies. During the night the Rus burned their dead, killed the prisoners in their honor, and offered sacrifices to the gods. The besieged were weakened by hunger. They made a last desperate attempt to break their way through. The Greek army wavered, and the emperor had to go into battle himself, at the head of his bodyguard—the "immortals". The sortie was repulsed; many of the Rus were wounded, and killed, and Svyatoslav himself was wounded. Further resistance was impossible. In 971 Svyatoslav concluded a peace treaty by which he surrendered Bulgaria. But the Greek government still feared Svyatoslav and informed the Pechenegs of his return to his native land. They ambushed Svyatoslav at the Dnieper rapids, where they killed him (972). The Pecheneg prince made a drinking cup of the skull of the murdered Svyatoslav.

CHAPTER 40

INTRODUCTION OF
CHRISTIANITY INTO KIEV RUS

VLADIMIR SVYATOSLAVICH
(980-1015)

Svyatoslav, during his absence at the wars, had left the government of his domains in the hands of his three sons. The land of the Polyane, including Kiev, went to his oldest son Yaropolk; the land of the Drevlyane (to Oleg) and Novgorod to Vladimir. soon after the death of their father, the brothers quarrelled. Oleg and Yaropolk fell in battle, and Vladimir again united all the lands of the Eastern Slavs under his rule. Subsequently he extended his possessions at the expense of his neighbors. Vladimir annexed the land of Galich (Halicz) to the Kiev state, and marched against the Poles, who wanted to take possession of it. Vladimir also advanced against Lithuania. But his chief concern was to defend his southern frontiers against the raids of the Pechenegs. During his rule the steppe borders were fortified with ramparts and palisades, forts were erected and warlike people were settled on the frontier.

CHAPTER 41

ADOPTION OF CHRISTIANITY

During Vladimir's reign, Kiev Rus adopted the Greek Orthodox religion, as Greek Christendom is called in distinction to that of Western Europe, called Catholicism. The Eastern Slavs became acquinted with Christian culture through their regular trade and political intercourse with Byzantium and their frequent trips to Constantinople. The chief reason for the adoption of Christianity was the fact that the class of feudal lords, which sprang up in the Dnieper region, needed a religion which would support it's class interests. Furthermore, the old heathen religion was in the hands of sorcerer-priests, representatives of the old tribal nobility, who were hostile to the princes. The first to embrace Christianity were the representatives of the upper class, including their retainers. Even under Igor there already were many Christians in the prince's military retinue. Igor's widow, Olga, had also adopted Christianity. At the end of the year 987, a revolt broke out in the Byzantine empire. At the same time the Danube Bulgars threatened Byzantium from the north. The Byzantine government called upon the Kiev prince for help. An alliance was formed (988) which was to be sealed by the baptism of Vladimir and the entire Russian people and by the marriage of the Kiev prince to the Greek Princess Anna (two emperors ruled Byzantium at that time; Princess Anna was their sister). With the help of a contingent of Russian troops, the revolt in Byzantium was suppressed. Byzantium, however, was in no hurry to fulfil the terms of the agreement concerning the marriage of Vladimir and Princess Anna. Vladimir besieged and took the city of Khersones (Korsun) in the Crimea, which belonged to Byzantium, and forced Byzantium to fulfil it's part of the treaty. Vladimir was baptized according to the rites of the Greek church and married Princess Anna.

On his return from Khersones, Vladimir ordered the whole

population of Kiev to be driven to the river, in which they were baptized by Greek priests. The images of the gods were burnt, and an idol of Peroun was thrown into the Dnieper. The population of other cities was baptized in the same way. Christianity, however, did not take immediate root. Heathen beliefs continued to prevail for a very long time, especially, among the rural population.

The adoption of Christianity was an important event in the life of Kiev Rus. In comparison with heathenism, Christianity was a great advance on the path of progress. It stimulated the further development and strengthening of feudal relations in Kiev Rus, since the Greek clergy employed peasant serfs on their church lands, and not slaves. The church advocated the liberation of the slaves.

Christianity was instrumental in spreading the higher Byzantine culture among the Eastern Slavs. The establishment of a single religion hastened the unification of all Slavonic tribes and strengthened the power of the princes.

The introduction of Christianity also brought about closer ties with Byzantium and the states of Western Europe. Vladimir maintained friendly relations with Czechia, Poland and Hungary. He became related to the Greek imperial house through his marriage with Anna. The cultural influence of the more enlightened Christian countries also increased. Kiev, in the manner of Byzantium, erected stone buildings ornamented with paintings and mosaic work. The heathen shrines gave way to a church built by Greek craftsmen, and beside it, a palace was erected for Vladimir.

Education became more widespread. About a hundred years before the conversion of Rus, the missionaries Cyril and Methodius, upon instructions from the Greek government, invented a Slavonic alphabet and translated the Greek scriptural books into the Slavonic (Bulgarian) dialect to facilitate the preaching of Christianity among the Western and Southern Slavs. Thanks to this, Kiev Rus, after it's conversion, received books in the Slavonic language. Vladimir ordered the children of the nobility to be taken from their parents and forcibly taught to read and write.

The memory of Vladimir has been preserved in folk songs or byliny. In these songs the people embodied their ideal of love for their native land in the persons of their valorous knights (Prince Vladimir's warriors, the peasant Ilya of Murom, Dobrynya Kikitich, Alyosha Popovich, and others who defended their Russian land against the dwellers of the steppes. These folk songs present the period of Kiev Rus as a brilliant epoch in Russian history.

CHAPTER 42

YAROSLAV MUDRY (THE WISE)

Vladimir died in 1015 and immediately after his death a fierce struggle broke out among his sons. One of them, Svyatopolk, seized the power in Kiev and slew his brothers, Boris, Gleb and Svyatoslav. Another son, Yaroslav Vladimirovich, who had been entrusted with the government of Novgodrod during his father's lifetime, attacked Svyatopolk. With the help of the people of Novgorod, he routed Svyatopolk, who fled to Poland to his father-in-law, Prince Boleslaus the Brave. This internecine warfare among the princes exposed the Russian frontiers to foreign aggressors. Boleslaus of Poland invaded Rus, defeated Yaroslav on the Western Bug, entered Kiev and placed Svyatolpolk on the throne. The indignation of the Russians was aroused against the Poles who engaged in plundering and banditry. When the latter dispersed through the towns and villages to take up their winter quarters, the population slew them. Boleslaus fled to Poland with the remnants of his army. Without the support of the Polish king, Svyatopolk suffered a decisive defeat at the hands of Yaroslav and the Novgorodians, and was killed while trying to make his escape. Yaroslav united Kiev and Novgorod under his rule (1019). However, his brother Mstislav Vladimirovich, ruler of the Tmutarakan principality on the Taman Peninsula, near the Caucasus, launched a campaign against him. Mstislav conquered Seversk Land and the city of Chernigov from Yaroslav. The Dnieper became the boundary between the possessions of these two brothers. After Mstislav's death (1036) Yaroslav re-annexed the land of Seversk to the Kiev state.

The reign of Yaroslav (1019-1054) was marked by the ultimate triumph of Christianity in Kiev Rus. It was during his rule that the church administration was organized, and a metropolitan appointed by the patriarch of Constantinople was placed at the head of the church of Kiev. It was also under Yaroslav that the Pechersk Monastery near Kiev came into existence. This monastery played a great part in the spread of learning among the ruling classes of Kiev Rus.

The Kiev state in Yaroslav's reign occupied a leading position among the states ofEurope in point of power and the high level of it's culture. Evidence of the close political ties that existed between Kiev Rus and the states of Western Europe is furnished by the matrimonial alliances formed by Yaroslav's family with foreign courts; his sister was married to the Polish prince, one of his daughters to the French king, another to the Norwegian, and a third to the Hungarian. Yaroslav frequently interfered in the affairs of Poland. Taking advantage of the turmoil that reigned in Poland after the death of Boleslaus, Yaroslav once more recovered the towns which had been lost after Vladimir's death in Galich Rus. Later Yaroslav supported his brother-in-law, the Polish prince, by sending troops to his aid. The last campaign against Constantinople (1043), which ended in failure, was undertaken during Yaroslav's rule under the leadership of his son Vladimir.

In the Baltic region, which was already becoming the object of attacks by Germans, Yaroslav built the city of Yuriev (Tartu in Esthonian) and extended his power over the Baltic peoples. He built a city on the Volga which he named Yaroslav. In the south Yaroslav was compelled to wage a hard struggle against the Pechenegs. He continued to fortify the frontier belt by building towns.

During Yaroslav's reign, the earliest code of laws was compiled under the name of Yaroslav's Pravda, which revealed influences of Christian Byzantine legislation. Yaroslav's Pravda reflected the tenacity of the old clan customs; for instance, it sanctioned the blood feud, which was confined to the members of the family, and was not applicable to the clan. "If one man shall kill another", Pravda said, "the brother shall avenge a brother, the son a father, the father a son, the nephew on the brother's or on the sister's side; if there be none to take revenge, then forty grivnas (a grivna was a bar of silver weighing approximately 200 grams) shall be paid for the murdered person". However, this obligation to seek revenge was imposed only on the next of kin and not on the entire clan, for by that time the clan had already fallen apart. During the reign of Yaroslav's sons the blood feud was abolished altogether.

Yaroslav's Pravda was later supplemented and revised during the reign of his sons and grandsons.

CHAPTER 43

THE CULTURE OF KIEV RUS

The cultural development of Kiev Rus in the 11th century was greatly influenced by Byzantium which was the most civilized country in Europe at the time. The Russians, however, did not simply borrow an alien culture; they molded it to the form of their own national art as well as that of Western Europe and Transcaucasia. An ancient Russian, native culture was created on Kiev soil which subsequently formed the basis of the national cultures of the Russian, Ukrainian and Byelorussian peoples.

A considerable number of books translated from the Greek in Bulgaria on the Danube made their appearance in Kiev Rus together with the new religion. The prince and rich people had transcripts of these books made for themselves. Other books were translated anew into the Russian language.

Besides theological books there were secular writings, such as the Greek chronicles. Translated literature served as the model for original Russian works. The first attempts to compile a history of Rus date back to the time of Yaroslav. After his death these historical notes were elaborated in the Pechersk Monastery in the form of a voluminous work which related "whence came the Russian land". The underlying idea of this work was that of a united Russia and a united ancient Russian people. The volume "Nachalnaya Letopis" (Initial Annals) as it was commonly called, was composed of stories biographies of the princes, annual recordings of events made in various cities, passages from Greek chronicles, etc.

The Initial Annals have come down to us under the name, "Chronicle of Ancient Years", in the revised versions dated 1116 and 1118. The Initial Annals are the source of our information on the ancient history of the Dnieper region and it's adjacent lands. They are evidence of a high degree of learning in the monasteries of Kiev Rus and of the versatility and wealth of the translated and original literature of the times.

Byzantine influence made itself felt in art as well. During Yaroslav's reign the St. Sophia Cathedral was built in Kiev by Greek architects; however, the usual type of Byzantine architecture was modified to correspond to Russian tastes and demands. The St. Sophia Cathedral is a masterpiece of 11th century Russian art. The interior of the cathedral contains remarkable mosaics and fresocs. The so-called "Golden Gate" was also built during Yaroslav's rule. Foreigners were amazed at the splendor of Kiev and called it "the rival of Constantinople". Other cities, especially Novgorod, built similar magnificent structures. Vladimir, son of Yaroslav, built the superb St. Sophia Cathedral in Novgorod after the Kiev model.

Kiev became the center for Cossack crossroads. Kiev gave birth to the Ukraine. The Ukraine began to build around Kiev. Which brings us up to the 17th century and the life of Mazepa. But before we get into Mazepa, let's look at the Ukraine in the 17th century.

CHAPTER 44

THE UKRAINE IN THE 17TH CENTURY UNDER POLISH DOMINION

Seizure of Ukrainian and Byelorussian Lands By The Polish Gentry

After the conclusion of the Lublin Union between Lithuania and Poland in 1569, a large part of Ukrainian territory (the lands of Volhynia, Kiev, and Chernigov) passed to Poland. The big Polish landed gentry energetically set about helping themselves to Ukrainian and Byelorussian lands. At first they seized the lands of Western Ukraine, but at the end of the 16th century, they crossed to the left bank of the Dnieper. Large holdings of Polish magnates, the Zolkiewskis, Potochkis, and others, were formed on Ukrainian territory.

The rapid development of agriculture among the Polish landlords followed increased exports of corn from Poland and Lithuania to Western Europe. Corn from the estates was shipped by water to the ports of the Baltic Sea, the most important of which was Danzig. The condition of the peasants in Poland at that time was worse than in any other European country. The Polish landlords destroyed the peasant communities, which had large sections of land at their disposal. The Polish gentry seized the best community lands, settled the peasants on small plots and imposed heavy taxes and duties upon them. They introduced Polish methods and customs on their Ukrainian and Byelorussian estates.

The Polish landlord enjoyed unlimited power over the population on his estates. He could with impunity appropriate the peasant's property, inflict whatever punishment he saw fit, and even take his life. The peasants dared not complain to anyone about their persecution or wrongs. The landlords contemptuously called the peasants slaves and cattle.

The Poles suppressed the Ukrainian and Byelorussian national culture. The Polish gentry made use of the Catholic church to strengthen their own position in the Ukraine and in Byelorussia. The spread of Catholicism met with strong resistance from both the peasants and the city population, and some of the Ukrainian and Byelorussian landlords. Thereupon, on the proposal of the Jesuits, a plan was drawn up for the union of the Catholic and Orthodox churches. According to this union, most of the church rituals of the Orthodox believers were to remain unchanged, but the Orthodox church was to be brought under the Papal authority. A church assembly was convened in the city of Brest in 1596 to settle the question of effecting this union. The majority of the assembly were opposed to a union and insisted on the complete independence of the Orthodox church. Their will, however, was overruled by the minority who, despite the opposition, proclaimed the union, which was confirmed by a special edict of the Polish king. The object of the union was to help subordinate the Ukrainian and Byelorussian lands to Poland, and signified the further intensification of Polish-Papal aggression against Russia.

The urban population also suffered from Polish oppression. In the 15th and 16th centuries many Ukrainian and Byelorussian cities had been granted self-government. With the growth of Polish land tenure in the Ukraine and Byelorussia, the cities became dependent upon Polish authority and the Polish landlords. According to Polish law, all landlords had the right to export the products of their estates and to buy whatever goods they needed duty-free. This privilege dealt a serious blow to city trade. The Polish authorities set aside the cities' rights to self-government; the Polish landlords seized the city lands and hampered the crafts and trade.

The Ukrainian and Byelorussian population in the cities united in "brotherhoods", organized under the churches, which fought for the preservation of their national culture and waged war against the Catholic church. The brotherhoods opened their own schools and printing shops, published books, and rendered assistance to their needy members. Some of the Ukrainian and

Byelorussian feudal lords copied the Polish gentry and nobles, adopted the Polish language and Polish customs and usages; but the mass of the people remained true to their native language and country, and the Poles were unable to destroy the national culture of the Ukraine and Byelorussia.

The Ukrainian and Byelorussian peasants, to escape the oppression of the Polish landlords, went south, to the still unsettled steppes of the Lower Dnieper. At the same time Russian peasants, to escape the oppression of the Russian landlords, migrated to the Don. A fortified camp of Cossacks and runaway peasants from the Ukraine was organized on the Island of Khortitsea, near the Dnieper falls. These people came to be called the Zaporozhye (backfalls) Cossacks. Abatises of hewn trees were erected as protection against attacks, whence these fortified Cossack camps came to be called Sech, from the Russian word for abatis. The chief pursuits of the Cossacks were fishing, hunting, and various crafts. The cossacks often waylaid the Tatars returning home to the Crimea after their raids and recaptured their captives and booty. As a reprisal against Turkish and Tatar inroads on Ukrainian lands the Cossacks carried out raids on the Crimea and Turkish towns situated on the Black Sea coast. Zaporozhye practically had no permanent population. The Cossacks gathered at the Sech early in the spring when the high tide had fallen. At such times the island became a noisy, populous camp. The Cossacks elected an ataman and other military captains. Hundreds of people were busy building the long Cossack row-boats of willow and linden, called "gulls", repairing their weapons and putting in a stock of provisions. When all preparations had been completed, large numbers of Cossack boats would move swiftly down the Dnieper out into the Black Sea. Usually the Cossacks made for Turkish shores, sometimes reaching the very capital of the sultan (Constantinople). The Cossacks crossed the sea so quickly that the Turkish sentry posts rarely had a chance to warn the sultan of the imminent danger. The strength of the Cossacks lay in the daring and unexpectedness of their attack. In the winter, the Zaporozhskaya Sech was deserted. The Cossacks left for Ukrainian and Polish cities where they sold the booty they had obtained on their raids and their own products.

Only guards remained on Khortitsa Island. Cannon, firearms, boats, etc., were carefully hidden away until the following spring.

At the end of the 16th century, the number of Zaporozhye Cossacks increased considerably. Under King Stephen Bathory part of the Cossacks were entered in special lists (registers) and were called "registered Cossacks". The Polish government endeavoured to use them to defend the frontier Polish lands and for purposes of war. The "registered Cossacks" therefore received a salary from the king and were quartered in the cities. Only an insignificant number of Cossacks, consisting of the more wealthy elements, were included in the register. It was the intention of the Polish government to make serfs of the other Cossacks and return them to the landlords.

At the end of the 16th century, a process of class stratification set in among the registered Cossacks, with the appearance of an upper stratum of petty landed proprietors, who acquired their own homesteads, had their own serfs and owned various industries.

The registered Cossack troops were under the command of a hetman, confirmed by the king, with a staff of chiefs, called the "general starshina", elected by the Cossacks and consisting of well-to-do members of the Cossack community.

CHAPTER 45

POPULAR UPRISINGS AGAINST POLAND

Polish oppression in the Ukraine and Byelorussia evoked a number of spontaneous popular outbreaks at the end of the 16th century. In these uprisings the Zaporozhye Cossacks usually joined forces with the peasant rebels. Sometimes a part of the registered Cossacks also joined them. During the uprisings the peasants set fire to Polish castles and killed the landlords, who, if they managed to escape, fled to Poland, whence they returned with Polish troops and cruelly avenged themselves on the peasants. The rebels sought refuge in the vast, dense forests along the middle reaches of the Dnieper, from where they waged a protracted partisan warfare.

The first big insurrections took place in the nineties of the 16th century. In 1595, Severin Nalivaiko, the son of a fur-dresser, headed a rebellion which broke out in Volhynia. Nalivaiko's detachments moved to Byelorussia and stirred up the Byelorussian peasants. The rebels captured several cities: Slutsk, Mogilev and Pinsk.

The Polish king, Sigismund III, sent a large army under Hetman Zolkiewski to suppress the uprising. Nalivaiko's detachment was surrounded near the city of Lubny. During an armistice the Poles treacherously killed the disarmed people and transported the leader of the uprising, Nalivaiko, to Warsaw, where he was tortured to death. The peasant movement against the Polish gentry continued into the beginning of the 17th century.

In the thirties of the 17th century the Zaporozhskaya Sech rose up once more against the Poles. The uprising was suppressed owing to the treachery of the elders. After this the Poles, with the help of a French engineer, built the fortress of Kodak above the falls to prevent Zaporozhye from having any intercourse with the Ukraine. The Polish hetman invited the Cossacks to look at the fortification that had been put up against them.

"What do you think of Kodak?" he asked mockingly.

"What human hands have built human hands will destroy," Bogdan Khmelnitski, the chief of a Cossack hundred, replied to him.

A few years later another uprising occurred, during which the Cossacks actually destroyed the fortress of Kodak.

Not until 1638, however, did the Polish troops succeed in crushing the popular rebellion in the Ukraine. The Polish Diet abolished "for all time" all Cossack privileges and self-government. The hetman was replaced by a commissary of the Polish government. The number of registered Cossacks was reduced. They were placed under the command of the szlachta, the Ukrainian cities were garrisoned by Polish troops.

CHAPTER 46

THE STRUGGLE OF THE UKRAINIAN PEOPLE AGAINST POLAND

BOGDAN KHMELNITSKI

After the rebellion of 1638 was suppressed there were no new peasant outbreaks in the Ukraine and Byelorussia for a period of ten years. Punitive expeditions of the Polish szlachta went deep into the Ukraine, on the left bank of the Dnieper, and the resistance of the peasants was broken. The Polish nobles called this a time of "golden peace." However, the hatred of the oppressed Ukrainian and Byelorussian population for the Polish power grew all the more intense.

In the spring of 1648 the Ukraine rose up once more against the oppression of the Polish entry and the power of Poland. The movement was initiated by the Zaporzhye Cossacks under the leadership of Bogdan Khmelnitski.

Bogdan Khmelnitski was a popular figure in the Ukraine. He was an educated person, had studied at the Kiev Academy, and knew the Latin language. He had more than once been participant and leader of daring Cossack campaigns. As far back as the 'twenties Bogdan had fought together with the Poles against the Turks, the common enemy of the Ukraine and Poland. Bogdan's father fell in the battle of Chechora near Jassy; Bogdan himself had been taken prisoner by the Turks who kept him in captivity for nearly two years. The Cossacks often elected him to carry on negotiations with the Polish government; at which times Bogdan defended the interests of the Cossacks.

Bogdan Khmelnitski was a prosperous Cossack and was included in the army register. His estate was situated not far from Chigirin. The dire condition of the Ukraine under Polish domination aroused Khmelnitski's indignation and wrath. Such indeed was the state of mind of many of the well-to-do registered Cossacks, who were better off than the peasants and rank-and-file Cossacks. Soon Bogdan Khmelnitski personally experienced the savage tyranny of the Polish authorities. A Polish squire by the name of Chaplinski unlawfully obtained an investiture from the Polish authorities to Khmelnitski's estate, suddenly took possession of his homestead and put Khmelnitski's whole household in chains. When Bogdan Khmelnitski sought justice against the offender, Chaplinski flogged Khmelnitski's ten-year-old son to death. Khmelnitski likewise failed to obtain redress at the king's court. This incident strikingly demonstrated to the Cossack elder the defenceless state of the Ukrainian people at the mercy of arbitrary Polish rule.

Returning home after his failure to obtain justice at Warsaw, Bogdan Khmelnitski gathered his Cossack friends in a secret conference, at which he called upon them, for the first time, to raise a rebellion against Polish domination.

"Can we leave our brothers in such distress?" he asked. "I have seen dreadful persecution everywhere. Our unhappy people ask for help".

The old Cossacks replied: "It is time to take up the sword, time to throw off the Polish yoke."

The Polish gentry, learning of Khmelnitski's plans through some traitors, imprisoned him. Khmelnitski succeeded in escaping to Zaporozhye, where he fortified himself on one of the islands. Meanwhile, peasant outbreaks had begun in the Ukraine. There was not a village or hamlet where the call to rise was not heard. One Polish squire confiscated several thousand firearms which had been hidden by his peasants. The gentry hastily left their castles, abandoning their property, and fled to Poland. There was every sign of an imminent general uprising in the Ukraine.

Bogdan Khmelnitski realized that the struggle against the well-armed, numerous Polish troops would be a difficult one. He therefore hit on the expedient of forming an alliance with the Crimean khan. Khmelnitski left Zaporozhye for the capital of the Crimea—Bakhchisarai. At that time the Crimean khan's displeasure was roused against the Polish king, who had not paid him any tribute for several years. The khan sent a body of Tatars with Khmelnitski under the command of one of his princes. Zaporozhskaya Sech welcomed Bogdan's return from the Crimea with acclamation, and at an assembly of the Cossacks proclaimed him the hetman's office (the bulava, or baton).

In the spring of 1648, Khmelnitski and his Cossacks set forth from Zaporozhye. The Polish troops under Hetman Potocki went out to meet them. In the beginning of May, Khmelnitski defeated a detached Polish army corps at Zheltiye Vody (Yellow Waters). The Cossacks serving in this corps had gone over to Khmelnitski before the battle started. News of the defeat caused Potocki to beat a hasty retreat. Khmelnitski pursued the enemy, and in the middle of May completely routed him at Korsun. Hetman Potocki was taken prisoner. The Cossacks and Tatars obtained rich booty.

CHAPTER 47

THE UPRISINGS OF THE PEASANTS

The victories over the Polish troops won by the Cossacks under Bogdan Khmelnitski were followed by a wave of peasant uprisings that spread throughout the Ukraine. Landlords abandoned their castles and property and fled to Poland. The rebellious peasants found brave leaders in their own midst, notable among whom as Maxim Krivonos, or as he was called in folklore, Perebiinos (Broken Nose). Jeremiah Wisniowiecki, a rich Polish Ukrainian magnate, used incredibly cruel means in his attempt to crush the rebellion. But he was unable to withstand the encounter with the Cossack-peasant detachments led by Maxim Krivonos, who appeared with astonishing rapidity at rallying points of the Polish gentry. The Ukraine was followed by Byelorussia, where dozens of peasant detachments were also formed. A contingent of Byelorussian peasants under Krivoshapka operated daringly and effectively.

Bogdan Khmelnitski started his war with Poland in the

interests of the registered Cossacks. He demanded from Poland that she increase the number of registered Cossack troops, restore the Cossacks the rights they had been deprived of, pay up overdue salaries, and cease her persecution of the Orthodox church. The mass uprising of the peasants and the support rendered by the urban population showed Khmelnitski that it was not the Cossacks alone who were fighting Poland, but the entire Ukrainian people. Bogdan Khmelnitski headed the liberation movement of the Ukrainian people.

Together with Maxim Krivonos, who had joined him, he inflicted another, even more terrible defeat upon the Polish royal troops in September 1648, on the Pilyavka River.

The victory over the main Polish forces on the Pilyavka River opened the way to Warsaw before Khmelnitski. Khmelnitski continued his offensive, and driving the Poles before him out of the Ukraine, he advanced as far as Lvov and Zamostye, then returned to Kiev. The people acclaimed him as the liberator of the Ukraine from Polish bondage. After bearing a yoke for three hundred years, Kiev was liberated and returned to the Ukraine.

The Polish government sent envoys to Kiev to conclude peace, hoping thereby to gain time to collect a new army. Khmelnitski, bearing in mind the successes of the peasant uprisings, demanded that the Ukraine be freed of Polish troops. "I shall wrest the entire Ukrainian people from Polish captivity", he said to the Polish envoys. The peace negotiations came to nothing.

CHAPTER 48

THE ZBOROV PEACE

Khmelnitski opened a new campaign in the summer of 1649. He was joined by the Crimean khan, who came with a large Tatar force. Near the city of Zborov the Cossacks and Tatars surrounded the Polish troops. However, the Polish gentry succeeded in bribing the Crimean khan, who, upon receiving a large amount of gold from him, suggested to Khmelnitski that he conclude peace with the king. Appreciating the danger the Tatars represented in the event of his falling out with the khan, Khmelnitski consented and concluded a peace treaty which has become known as the Zborov Treaty. By this treaty part of the Ukraine was set up as the Zborov administration with it's own hetman, Bogdan Khmelnitski. The number of registered Cossacks was raised from 6,000 to 40,000.

With the conclusion of the Zborov Peac Treaty in 1649 ended the first state in the Ukraine's war of liberation. The peace terms satisfied the main demands of the rich registered Cossacks. It was otherwise, however, with the rank-and-file Cossacks and the peasants. Many peasants who had fought against the Polish gentry and had not been included among the 40,000 registered troops provided for by the peace treaty, had to return to their former places, to their former owners. The peasants remained as of old feudal serfs of the landlords. After the conclusion of peace the Polish gentry began to return to their Ukrainian estates. The Zborov Peace Treaty did not satisfy the peasants, who therefore did not wish to cease their struggle and refused to let the gentry return to their estates.

CHAPTER 49

RENEWAL OF WAR

Poland regarded the Zborov Peace as a respite which it needed for reorganizing its defeated army. The gentry also took advantage of this respite to crush the peasant movement. The fields were strewn with the corpses of peasants and city people, who had been tortured and murdered. Many peasant leaders lost their lives, among them Maxim Krivonos. In the beginning of 1651 Polish troops invaded the western region of the Ukraine before Khmelnitski had a chance to assemble his Cossacks to repel the attack. The valiant Nechai fell in the beginning of the new war.

In the spring of 1651, a large Polish army headed by the king took the field. The Pope absolved of their sins all those who took part in the war against the Ukrainian people. Khmelnitski once more joined forced with the Crimean khan. The battle began in June 1651, near Berestechko, but during the course of the fighting the Tatars suddenly deserted the Cossacks and withdrew.

Bogdan Khmelnitski hastened to the khan to urge him to return to the battlefield. But the khan not only did not return, but detained the hetman. The Cossacks and peasants, left leaderless, entrenched themselves in their camp and for several days bravely repelled the attacks of the Poles. Bogun, known alike to the Cossacks, elected him as their leader. He organized allies and amazed the enemy by his military cunning and the daring of his unexpected attacks.

However, the forces were unequal, and the necessity of effecting a withdrawal became obvious to the Cossacks. During the night some of them left unnoticed by a wooden paving laid across the swamp. When dawn came the Poles rushed the camp, and wreaked cruel vengeance upon the few remaining defenders, among whom were many poorly-armed peasants. About three hundred Cossacks entrenhed themselves upon a small island and stubbornly continued to defend themselves. The Poles proposed that they surrender and promised to spare their lives, but the answer they got from the Cossacks was: "We do not hold our lives dear, and we abhor the favor of the enemy." Saying which the Cossacks embraced each other and rushed at the poles. All the Cossacks died the death of heroes.

It was not until a month later that the Crimean khan released Khmelnitski. By that time the Poles has taken Kiev, and the Tatars had ravaged the country ruthlessly. The hetman had to agree to the onerous terms of a peace treaty signed in the autumn of 1651 at Belaya Tserkov. Almost everything that had been won in hard struggle was now lost again. The number of registered Cossack troops was reduced to 20,000. The Cossacks were deprived of the rights they had received under the Zborov Peace Treaty.

When the Polish landlords returned to the Ukraine, they cruelly avenged themselves on the peasants for their participation in the struggle. Fleeing from persecution the peasants thronged to the left bank of the Knieper and pushed on further into the territory of the Russian state. The Ukrainian territory under Polish power became quickly deserted. Meanwhile the Ukrainian population colonized the fertile regions along the upper reaches of the Northern Donets, where dozens of new Ukrainian settlements sprang up. This region came to be called the "Slobodskaya Ukraina."

Despite the peace of Belaya Tserkov, detachment of the Polish gentry continued to pillage Ukrainian villages and settlements, to rob and kill the inhabitants, sparing neither old people, women, nor children. The Polish king made peace with the Crimean khan and gave him leave to despoil the Ukrainian population during a period of forty days. An endless stream of fettered captives filled the roads to the Crimea. The Crimeans carried off tens of thousands of men and women, doomed to a life of slavery. An ancient Ukrainian song says of those times:

> Ukraine's people grieving, they have nowhere to hide,
>
> The hordes of nomad horsemen o'er children's bodies ride,
>
> The tender babes they trample, the old they lead away, behind them shackled to be the dread khan's prey

CHAPTER 50

INCORPORATION OF THE UKRAINE INTO THE RUSSIAN STATE "WAR WITH POLAND"

The war of 1648-1651 clearly demonstrated that the Ukraine could not free herself from Polish bondage unaided. Surrounded as she was by more powerful states, there could be no question of securing independence at that time. Therefore, when, in 1652, the Ukrainian peasants and Cossacks rose a second time against the Polish landlords and the Polish power, Khmelnitski entered into negotiations with the Moscow government for the Ukraine's incorporation into the Russian state. At the Zemski Sobor assembled in Moscow in the autumn of 1653 Russia decided to take the Ukraine under her protection and to declare war on Poland. On January 8, 1654, the Rada, i.e., the conference of representatives of the Ukraine Cossacks, met in Pereyaslavl, with

Moscow envoys attending. Hetman Bogdan Khmelnitski addressed the assembled Cossacks, reminding them of the difficult position the Ukrainian people were in.

"You all know", he said, "that our enemy wishes to exterminate us so thoroughly, that even the name Rus (i.e., Ukrainian) will never again be mentioned in our land. Therefore, select on of four rulers for yourselves. The first is the Turkish sultan; he oppresses the Greeks. The second is the Crimean khan; he has shed the blood of our brothers many times; the third is the Polish king. There is no need to tell you of the persecution by the Polish gentry. The fourth is the tsar of great Rus, the Eastern tsar."

Thousands of voices replied: "We will (i.e., wish) to be under the Eastern tsar."

Under an agreement concluded somewhat later in Moscow the Ukraine received the right of self-government, headed by an elected hetman. The number of registered Cossacks was set at 60,000.

It was much more difficult for the Ukrainian people to tolerate the rule of the Polish king and Polish landlords than to be subjects of the Russian tsar. The Velikorussi (Great Russians) were kin to the Ukrainian and Byelorussian peoples by origin, language and culture. The Ukraine's incorporation into the Russian state signified a reunion of two great fraternal peoples which was to save the Ukraine from seizure by Poland and Turkey.

CHAPTER 51

WAR WITH POLAND AND SWEDEN

Poland was unwilling to relinquish the Ukraine to Russia. Only war, therefore, could liberate the Ukraine from Polish domination. In Moscow it was decided to begin a war with Poland for both the Ukraine and Byelorussia. The war broke out in 1654 and continued, with intermissions, for thirteen years (1654-1667). During the very first year of the war almost the entire territory of Byelorussia was liberated from Polish oppression. In many cities the residents themselves drove out the Polish garrisons. The population greeted the Russian troops with joy. In the autumn Smolensk surrendered. the following summer Russian troops occupied Vino. At the same time Ukrainian and Russian troops waged a successful struggle in the region west of the Dnieper against the Poles, and the Tatars who had gone over to their side. After liberating the Ukrainian lands, Bogdan Khmelnitski and the Muscovy warlords crossed the Polish frontier and took possession of Lublin.

In 1656, the Swedish king, Charles X, intent on seizing certain regions of Poland, intervened in the war. He occupied Warsaw, Cracow, and many other Polish cities. Swedish aggression induced the Polish government to start peace negotiations with Muscovy. In the interests of a lasting peace, the government of Muscovy demanded of the Polish envoys the relinquishment of the Ukraine and Byelorussia. Since, however, Poland did not agree to these terms, only a truce was signed, by the terms of which both sides ceased hostilities.

The struggle with Poland once more proved to Russia her need of Baltic ports in order to maintain relations with Western Europe, whence she received arms and military supplies. The government of Muscovy decided to make an attempt to wrest from Sweden the southern shore of the Baltic Sea, which the latter had seized in the first half of the 17th century. The war with Sweden started in 1656. The Russian army captured several Swedish fortresses on the Western Dvina and besieged Riga. The siege was a failure, inasmuch as the garrison of the Swedish fortress received reinforcement from the sea. The war dragged on for several years with alternating success. In 1661, the Treaty of Kardis was concluded; according to it's terms both sides retained their former possessions. This time, too, Russia failed to acquire an outlet to the Baltic Sea.

In 1657, Bogdan Khmelnitski died. His hetmanship had been recognized throughout the Ukraine. After his death a struggle for power broke out among the rival factions of Ukrainian elders. Poland took advantage of this conflict and tried to bribe the Ukrainian feudal lords, the elders and the rich Cossacks, with money and promises. The new hetman, Wigowski, a szlachcic by origin, and some of his Cossack elders went over to the side of Poland. In league with the Crimean khan he succeeded in defeating the Russian troops near Konotop. In violation of the truce the Polish troops also reopened hostilities. However, the rank-and-file Cossacks and the Ukrainian peasants did not support the Polish faction, but continued to fight manfully shoulder to shoulder with the Russian troops for the liberation of the Ukraine. Both sides, Poland and Russia, were greatly exhausted by the protracted war. At last, in 1667, after prolonged negotiations, the Truce of Andrusovo, near Smolensk) for 13-1/2 years. Russia retained part of Byelorussia, Smolenski, and the Ukrainian lands on the left bank of the Dnieper. On the right bank of the Dnieper Russia acquired Kiev and the adjoining district for two years, but it did not return this land to the Poles upon the expiry of this period. In 1686, the Poles had to agree to the union of Kiev with Russia in perpetuity.

Now that I've bored you up to this point on esoteric history of the Ukrainian people, let me introduce you to the subject of this research; MAZEPA.

CHAPTER 52

ORGANS OF GOVERNMENT OF THE RUSSIAN STATE

THE POWER OF THE TSAR

The state structure of Russia as a system of feudal serfdom took final form in the 17th century under the Romanovs. In order to maintain his domination, in order to retain his power, the landlord had to have an apparatus which would unite, under his rule, a tremendous number of people and would subordinate them to certain laws and regulations, and all these laws essentially boiled down to one, the retention of power by the landlord over the serf. At the head of the Russian state was an autocratic tsar who was himself the first and foremost landlord of the realm. The nobles had need of a strong tsar, who could protect their class interests.

The will of the tsar was law for the entire land. All military servitors, even the aristocratic boyars, called themselves the servants of the tsar; and assessed people (the townsfolk and peasants) could not even call themselves that. They were the tsar's "little orphans". When addressing the tsar, everyone had to refer to himself in the diminutive: Petrushka, Ivashka (Peterkin, Johnny). They did obeisance to the tsar as to a deity, touching the ground with their foreheads.

The tsar's power was also sustained by the splendor with which he surrounded himself. On ceremonious occasions, when receiving foreign ambassadors or attending church, the tsar appeared in sumptuous "full-dress", in a brocaded kaftan embroidered in pearls, the royal shoulder-mantle richly ornamented with images of the saints, the Monomakh cap, and a scepter in his hands.

CHAPTER 53

THE RUSSIAN STATE BEFORE
THE PEASANT WAR

SERFDOM

In the second half of the 16th century, the lot of the peasants became a very hard one. The landed proprietors, who were in financial straits, extended seignorial tilths and increased taxation of the peasants in money and kind. Formerly the extent of the peasant's servile tenures had been fixed by custom; the peasant tilled the seignorial land and paid his quitrent "as of old". Ignoring this established tradition, the landlords, in the 16th century, themselves determined the payments and tenures of their peasants. The royal proclamations required the peasants to obey their landlords in all things, to do whatever the landlords told them to do, pay their quitrent, etc.

Great expenditures had been incurred by the Livonian war. The monetary taxes imposed on the peasants and the urban trading population and craftsmen were increased manifold. Seeking to escape from oppressive labor, taxation and starvation, the peasants left their homes and villages "en mase" and went to the east, beyond the Volga; even more went south, beyond the Oka River, where lay the almost uninhabited black-earth steppe, and where a fugitive peasant could not easily be found. This migration of the peasants caused a serious void in the central regions.

Deprived of labor hands the feudal estates of the landlords found themselves in a difficult plight. The landowners who suffered from a shortage of hands competed with others in trying to attract settlers to their lands. Every year on the eve of St. George's Day this keen competition for peasant labor opened up anew. Most of the peasants lacked the money to settle accounts with their landlords. The bailiffs of competing landlords would then make the settlement on their behalf and convey the peasants to the estates of their new masters. Rich, powerful landowners would even organize raids on their neighbors' estates, and carry off the peasants in chains to their new domicile. The lower and middle ranks of the nobles complained that they were unable to render the military service required of their depopulated estates.

In 1581, during the defense of Pskov, Tsar Ivan IV temporarily, "pending the royal ukase" prohibited peasants to migrate on St. George's Day. The year when the peasants were forbidden to change their domicile even on St. George's Day was called the first "Zapovedni" year (year of interdict). The peasants were still more strongly fettered to the soil of the landlords.

CHAPTER 54

THE COSSACKS

With the growth of serfage in the central regions of Russia there occurred a notable swelling of the ranks of the Cossacks at the end of the 16th century, due to the influx of the Russian population to the outskirts of the country—to the upper reaches of the Oka, the Bryansk forests and to the Don. The steppe, which abounded in wild fowl, and the rivers teeming with fish could sustain a relatively large population on the Don. The Cossacks felt safe here from the tyranny of the landlords and the tsar's waywodes. They did not engage in agriculture, but imported corn from Russian cities.

The Cossacks fought against Tatar and Turkish domination on the Azov and Black seas; when in luck they obtained good booty, which they divided among themselves. Sometimes the Cossacks also robbed Russian merchants on the Volga. All matters of common interest concerning expeditions, the division of spoil and relations with Moscow, were decided by the Cossacks at a meeting which was called "krug" (circle). At these "krugs" they also elected their chiefs (atamans).

CHAPTER 55

MAZEPA & PETER THE GREAT

Ivan Stepanovitch Mazepa, the son of a nobleman of the orthodox faith from the western part of Little Russia, or the Ukraine, was born about 1645. The family was well-known in the country, and in 1597 one of his ancestors had, together with the unfortunate Hetman Nalivaiko, been roasted alive by the Poles. A handsome youth, well educated in a Jesuit school, he was appointed page at the court of King Jan Casimir. Although the victories of the Cossacks had compelled the Poles to make a few concessions to the Ukrainians, yet Catholic fanaticism was rampant, and the comrades of Mazepa taunted him so often about his religion and his nationality that one day he impatiently drew his sword. Such an act in the royal palace was a capital offense, but the King, taking into account the circumstances of the case, merely exiled Mazepa from the court. He withdrew to his mother's estate in Volynia, where he became engaged in an intrigue with the wife of a neighboring nobleman, Falbowski. On one of his visits he was waylaid by the injured husband, was ignominiously stripped and bound to his horse. The spirited animal, frightened by the cuts of a whip and the firing of a pistol close to his ear, rushed furiously through woods and thickets, and brought his master home so torn and bleeding that he was hardly recognisable. Unable to meet his equals after such an adventure, Mazepa sought a refuge among the Cossacks, where he took service first under the Hetman Tetera and subsequently under Doroshenko. As in addition to Polish and Russian he knew German and Latin, he soon rose to the important position of Secretary-General, and in 1674 was sent to the Cossacks of the

Russian side of the Dnieper with a proposition of Doroshenko for annexation. Doroshenko afterwards sent him to Constantinople to ask the aid of the Sultan, but he was captured by the Ataman of the Zaporovian Cossacks, who sent him to Moscow. The boyar Matveief had charge of the examination, and was pleased with the bearing of Mazepa, who professed himself favorably disposed to Russia, and tried to exculpate Doroshenko. He was pleased, presented to the Tsar, and sent back with friendly messages. He preferred, however, to remain with the Hetman Samoilovitch, and received permission to live in the Russian Ukraine. Samoilovitch confided to him the education of his children, and soon raised him to the dignity of Yesaul General, the next rank after that of Hetman. He was frequently sent to Moscow on commissions, and while there succeeded in ingratiating himself with Prince Basil Golitsyn, who was at that time all powerful. Golitsyn and Matveief, both of whom had respect for the education given in Poland and Ukraine, so far superior to that of Moscow, were captivated by Mazepa's intelligence and manners. When Samoilovitch became the scapegoat of the unfortunate Crimean campaign in 1687, and was deposed, Golitsyn made Mazepa his successor.

CHAPTER 56

MAZEPA'S RELATIONS WITH GOLITSYN

Mazepa continued his friendly relations with Golitsyn. And at the time of the overthrow of Sophia had just arrived at Moscow for the purpose of presenting himself personally to the Government. As we have already related, he succeeded in clearing himself of any complicity with Sophia, and in ingratiating himself with Peter. Political necessities demanded Mazepa's retention as Hetman, and the charm of his manners and the apparent simplicity and openness of his character inspired Peter with a confidence in him that remained unshaken in spite of rumors and accusations, until he actually went over to the Swedish camp.

It is in the sixteenth century that we must fix the rise of the Cossacks as a class. In the middle of that century they made their appearance on the outskirts of Russia in most opposite localities: on the confines of Poland, on the Don and the southern border, and on the extreme east. They were at first nothing but the vagabonds and men not bound to the soil by the fixed ties of serf labor, such as were to be found in every village. Following the Russian proverb, "The fish seeks where it is deepest and the man where it is best", they made their way to the confines of the empire to get rid of compulsory work for the lords of the soil and to be free in the widest sense of the term. The word Cossack, or Kazak, is of Tartar origin, meaning, first, a free, homeless vagabond, and then one of the partisans and guerilla warriors formed out of such vagabonds. This signification of the name was never quite lost, and even when the Cossacks were preeminently the military colonies and brotherhoods on the frontiers, their name was in popular parlance given to robber bands. The Cossacks were a characteristic manifestation of the time—a national protest against the governmental forms which did not satisfy the Russian ideal. The ideal of the Cossacks was full personal freedom, unconditional possession of the soil, an elective government, popular justice administered by themselves, complete equality between the members of the society, contempt of all privileges of rank or birth, and mutual defense against external enemies. The neighborhood of the Tartars and of the other hostile tribes compelled the Cossacks to preserve a military organization. The fact that their enemies were non-Christian only increased their own love of religion and orthodoxy. That they themselves were discontented with the form of government in Russia made them always more or less hostile and suspicious of the central administration, even where they admitted its authority.

CHAPTER 57

THE DEVELOPMENT OF COSSACKS IN THE UKRAINE

The development of the Cossacks in the Ukraine was chiefly due to Dashkovitch and Landskoronski, Starosts or chiefs of towns in that region, who formed the inhabitants into a military class always ready to repulse the Tartar incursions. The successor of Dashkovitch, the enterprising Dimitri Wisniowiecki, received all volunteers who came to him, grew famous by the heroic victories of his Cossacks over the Crim Tartars, and became almost independent of the Polish crown. His plans for destroying the Crim Tartars failed through the obstinacy of the Tsar Ivan the Terrible. In 1563 the Cossacks had almost conquered Moldavia, when Wisniowiecki was treacherously captured by the Turks, tortured and killed.

The abundance of fish and wild animals below the long and dangerous cataracts of the Dnieper, which made navigation impossible, had early led many adventurers to settle themselves there in half military wise. Sitcha or Setch, which these Zaporovians (so called from their living za poroghi, beyond the cataracts) built on an island of the Dnieper, served at first simply as a refuge; but the peculiar rules of the brotherhood, for such it must be called, which made orthodoxy and celibacy obligatory, which forbade the presence of women in the settlement, which imposed severe tests on the candidate for initiation, and which put a premium on bravery and endurance, all tended to excite a martial spirit. During the first one hundred and fifty years of their existence the Zaporovians numbered scarcely more than three thousand, but at the end of the sixteenth century Setch could boast as many as twenty or thirty thousand braves.

In this way the Cossacks divided into two branches, those of the towns, or the Ukraine, who on account of their settled habitations were obliged to recognize the Polish authority, and the Zaporovians, who, although they owed a nominal allegiance to the Hetman of the Ukraine, were practically independent siding sometimes with the Turks, sometimes with the Tartars, and sometimes with their own countrymen. A close bond of union was nevertheless kept up between them, and many of the younger, braver and more restless from the Ukraine would go to Setch to pass a few years or their whole life among the Zaporovians.

The Polish nobles did much to extend the Cossacks, not foreseeing what dangerous results would follow for Poland. They themselves were Cossack leaders, and took them on their expeditions, and even the Polish kings used their services. Stephen Batori registered the Cossacks, put them under the command of a Hetman, and divided them into six regiments. The registered Cossacks, who had the freehold of their lands and paid no taxes, were 6,000 in number, and the Government refused to recognize any others. This did not suit the popular view. All the common people sought to be Cossacks or freemen, and one method of obtaining this object was by running away to Setcha. The Polish serf was in every sense of the word a slave, so entirely was he in the power of his lord. Where, as in the Ukraine, his lord was generally of an alien race and of another religion, his fate seemed doubly hard. When, therefore, he saw in his immediate neighborhood a free and independent class of his countrymen, he naturally tried to join them and get for himself the same rights. The runaway peasant, on returning from the Zaporovians, no longer wished to obey his lord, but claimed a right to the land on which he had lived and worked, and to be considered in every way as a Cossack. The proprietors caught such runaways when they could, and even put them to death. If persecuted in their former homes, there were always other lords who, for the sake of their service, were glad to give them protection and land. But on the slightest provocation they were as willing to treat their new protector in the same way as their former lord. The registered Cossacks showed no desire to limit their class, and in this way the actual number of Cossacks greatly exceeded the legal number. The lists were inspected form time to time, and such newcomers were stricken off; they then collected themselves into bands, elected their Hetmans, and continued to call themselves Cossacks, and although legally they were considered mere marauders, yet the nobles at times used them in their wars with Muscovy, Sweden and Turkey. In 1646 over 2,000 Cossacks went to France and served in the siege of Dunkirk.

The tendency of the people to become Cossacks received a religious coloring, and in their own eyes a moral consecration. After the union of the orthodox with the Catholic Church in Lithuania and Poland, the Russian proprietors rapidly went over to Catholicism, losing at the same time their nationality and becoming Poles in feeling. The townspeople and serfs accepted the union only on compulsion, and did not become accustomed to it for generations. In the Ukraine, where the people were bolder and less submissive, the Union made little progress. The registered

Cossacks, not fearing the landed proprietors, refused to receive it. The self-styled Cossacks hated it still more, as one of the marks of the hated rule of the lords. In this way the orthodox religion became for the Russians of the Ukraine an ensign of freedom and opposition to the nobility.

The concurrent testimony of all contemporary writers shows that at the end of the fifteenth and the beginning of the sixteenth centuries, the poor peasants of this region were reduced to a most miserable condition by the tyranny of their masters.

CHAPTER 58
ZAPOROVIAN COSSACKS

With the impulse given by the Zaporovians, rebellion succeeded to rebellion, accompanied on both sides by the most frightful barbarities. The Cossacks of the Ukraine turned their eyes to Moscow, the head of orthodoxy. Finally, under the lead of Bogdan Khmelnitzky, they succeeded in becoming "de facto" independent of Poland, and put themselves under the protection of the Tsar. This was in 1654.

With time, the circumstances, with the increase of wealth, and with the tendency to a more settled life, great changes had taken place in Little Russia or Ukraine. There had come into existence a land-owning class and a class of peasants who cultivated the great estates, whose interests were opposed to those of the genuine Cossacks, the adventurous fighting class. The Cossacks, supported and aided by the Zaporovians, envied the rich and the powerful, wished to break up the great estates, and to reintroduce the primitive democratic equality. The colonels and leaders, many of whom had managed to get hold of large estates when the Polish landlords had been driven out, chafed at their subjection to the Hetman, but at the same time wished to be independent of the Cossacks of the army. They, therefore, willingly assisted the Russians in registering the Cossacks, and thus prevented their increasing beyond a fixed number, so as to keep as many workmen as possible on their estates. The peasantry suffered from the exactions both of the landowners and of the fighting Cossacks, but sympathized rather with the latter. They all wished to leave their own conditions of life and become free Cossacks. The townspeople leaned towards any strong government that would protect them. Some were for the Poles and some for the Russians. Mazepa, with his Polish education and habits, naturally inclined to the side of the proprietors as against the purely military element, and in doing so not only carried out the views of the Moscow Government, but obtained support from it, and was able to bring in additional Streltsi and troops for his protection. He thus succeeded in maintaining his rule without any open outbreak; but, nevertheless, during the whole time of his Hetmanship The Ukraine was in a continual state of ferment. The bonds which then united the Ukraine to Moscow were not of the strongest. The Ukraine, though possessing strong religious sympathies—for their attachment to the orthodox Church was as strong as ever—had not yet come to look upon the 'Moscols,' as they called them, as their own countrymen. Considerable autonomy still existed, and the general desire was for <u>independence.</u> The Russian protection had been accepted simply as a means of being secure from the Polish yoke; but none of the Hetmans since the union with Russia had ever been unwilling to coquet with Poles, Tartars, and Turks when there had seemed a chance of freeing themselves from Russian supremacy without coming under the strict rule of another country. The Russian union had brought its disadvantages as well as its advantages. Taxes had increased, fortifications had been erected on Cossack territory, Russian troops occupied portions of the country, and the military autonomy of the land had been infringed.

It seemed impossible for a Hetman to retain long his popularity with the democratic Cossacks. He was always accused of yielding too much to the Russians, and at the same time there were constant intrigues for his place. Personal and political animosities sometimes took the form of denunciations at Moscow. Vygofsky and Bruchovetsky, in spite of accusations, had been trusted by the Moscow Government, and both had betrayed it. Mnogogrieshny had fallen the victim of his denunciations, and Samoilovitch, the only Hetman who was thoroughly devoted to Russian interests, had been sacrificed to save Golitsyn's reputation.

CHAPTER 59

MAZEPA'S CONFIDENCE
IN CZAR PETER

Mazepa succeeded, as we have said, in retaining the confidence of the Tsar. Little credence was given to the accusations frequently brought against him of treason and of secret correspondence with the Poles. Even as early as 1689 Mazepa had been accused of correspondence with king Jan Sobieski for the reunion of the Ukraine with Poland. There was certainly a correspondence of some sort, but some of the letters were forged, and Mazepa sent to Moscow those which he received from Szumlianski, Bishop of Lemberg. The persons implicated were surrendered to him for punishment, and through this he succeeded in getting some of his worst enemies sent to Siberia, and the number of Russian troops increased. In 1691 Petrik, a hot-headed and active Cossack connected by marriage with Kotchubey, the Secretary-General of the Cossacks, fled to the Zaporovians, and afterwards to the Khan of the Crim Tartars, carrying with him some important papers. He endeavoured to do what Khmelnitzky had done before him, raise the Zaporovians and bring the Tartars into the Ukraine, promising to free the Ukraine and to exterminate all the nobility and rich people. Mazepa sent rich presents and great promises to the Zaporovians, and Petrik, when he raised the standard of insurrection, could enlist under it only some of the more headstrong Cossacks and a very few Tartars. He was repulsed without difficulty, and Mazepa earned the gratitude of Moscow, to which he had a still greater right on account of his action with regard to spirit-farming. The farming of the liquor traffic was suspended for a year on trial, and taxes were imposed to meet the necessary deficiencies in the revenue. At the end of this time the population was glad enough to return to the old system. Indirect taxes seemed to press on them so much more lightly than direct imposts.

CHAPTER 60

MAZEPA'S ENEMY - SEMEN PALEI

A more dangerous rival and enemy of Mazepa was Semem Palei. After the death of Doroshenko, the population of the right bank of the Dnieper had been transferred to the Russian side, and by the treaty between Russia and Poland this region was to be left waste and uninhabited. The Poles very soon thought that it would be to their benefit to re-establish Cossacks in this region. No sooner had they done so than the Cossacks showed their natural tendency of opposing everything that was Polish and aristocratic. Palei led this sentiment, and used his influence to separate from Poland and to join the rest of the Ukraine under Muscovite protection. This he endeavoured to do through the mediation of Mazepa; but the Russian authorities had no wish to quarrel with Poland, and refused these offers. The Poles and Cossacks fought against each other with all the barbarity of indiscriminate slaughter and hideous executions which marked the warfare of that region and that day. Palei and his comrade Samus were driven out of some of their strongholds, but still kept possession of the town and province of Bielaya Tserkof. Mention has already been made of the efforts of the Poles to regain possession of this province. Palei was again and again summoned by Russia to submit to the Poles, and was urged to go first to the Zaporovians and then come to Russia, but he obstinately refused. Mazepa finally crossed the Dnieper, enticed Palei into his camp, took him prisoner, and gave him up to the Russians, who sent him to Siberia. Mazepa had a difficult part to play, for his own subjects all sympathized with Palei and the rebellious Cossacks of the other side, and he had himself befriended Palei, and had indeed always advised the Tsar to accept his offers of submission, and occupy this country which had been ceded to Poland. His action, therefore, in arresting Palei was viewed with great satisfaction by Peter. It was another proof of his unswerving loyalty, which was further shown in 1705, when, on receiving a letter from King Stanislas, he at once sent it to the Tsar with complaints that his enemies should thus for the fourth time dishonor him by the suspicions that he could be unfaithful to Russia.

CHAPTER 61

MAZEPA'S LOVE OF HIS GODCHILD

It was not long before Mazepa was again denounced, this time by a domestic enemy, the Judge-General Kotchubey, with whom there had been a family quarrel. Kotchubey had two daughters—Anna, the widow of Mazepa's nephew, and Matrena, who was his godchild. Mazepa was then a widower, and made proposals of marriage to Matrena, who was desperately in love with him. As such a marriage was against the laws of the Church, Kotchubey opposed it, and his wife began to treat the girl so harshly that she found it impossible to live longer at home, ran away, and took refuge with Mazepa. Wishing to avoid scandal, the Hetman sent her back to her father, as he afterwards wrote to her: 'Although I love no one on earth as much as you, and it would have been for me a happiness and joy to have had you come and live with me, I foresaw what the end of it might be, especially with such opposition and hatred on the part of your relatives. There would have been condemnation by the Church because we lived together; and what should I then have done with you? I should have been sorry if you had had cause to complain of me afterwards'. Matrena's situation on returning home was still worse than before, and she kept up a secret correspondence with Mazepa, whose love letters are interesting and curious. While assuring her of his love, he advised her as a last resource to take the veil in a convent. Kotchubey had his wife noised their troubles abroad, and finally, in reply to his accusations and complaints, Mazepa wrote: 'Pan Kotchubey: you write to tell about a heart's grief of yours, but you might better complain of your proud grandiloquent wife, whom, as I see, you will not or cannot control. She, and no one else, is the cause of your grief, if you have any. St. Barbara ran away from her father, not to the house of the Hetman, but to the woods, to shepherds, and to steep rocks, on account of her fear. You will never be free from your grief, and settled in prosperity, as long as you do not drive out of your heart that rebellious spirit of yours, which is not in you so much by nature as inspired by your wife. And if any misfortune has happened to you or to your house, you should complain only of the accursed pride and haughtiness of yourself and your wife. For sixteen years have I passed over your offenses, many though they were and grievous and worthy of death, but as I see, my patience and goodness have been all to no end. In your pasquiling letter you speak of an error, but I know and understand nothing except that you yourself fall into error when you listen to your wife. As is said in the proverb: "When the tail rules the head goes wrong." ' To Matrena he intimated that he would long ago have punished Kotchubey but for her sake.

Kotchubey in revenge resolved to accuse Mazepa of treason. A monk whom he sent to Moscow for that purpose was arrested and examined, but, as he could adduce no facts, the matter was not pursued further. Kotchubey then obtained the aid of his brother-in-law Iskra, the Colonel of Poltava, who denounced Mazepa to the Russian Colonel Osipof, commanding at Akhtyrka. The official reports reached the Tsar towards the end of March, 1708, and he at once wrote to Mazepa to express his entire disbelief in the whole story, as he was sure it was a machination of his enemies. Meanwhile, Kotchubey had sent another denunciation to Moscow, and of this Peter also informed the Hetman. At Mazepa's request, Kotchubey, Iskra, and Osipof, with several others, were arrested and taken to Vitebsk, where Kotchubey, in a long document containing thirty-three points, accused Mazepa of negotiations with the Swedes, and of treason against the Tsar. Annexed to this accusation was a patriotic ballad written by Mazepa. This ballad, of the kind called "duma" in the Ukraine, written in short trochaic lines, deplores the unhappy condition of Mother Ukraine, whose sons are divided by their own passions, and who suffers now from the Pole and now from the Russian. It exhorts the Ukrainians to union, to the defense of the country and of the faith. Neither this ballad nor any of the points of accusation stood the slightest examination, and, on the application of the usual torture, Kotchubey admitted that his accusation was false, and dictated by his desire for revenge. The Tsar thereupon sent Kotchubey and Iskra to Mazepa, and early in the morning of July 25, 1708 they were beheaded in the presence of the whole army of Cossacks and Ukrainians. Their property was confiscated.

Although the specific denunciations of Kotchubey were false and unsupported by proof, yet during this whole time Mazepa was engaged in secret correspondence with the Swedes.

The Cossacks sent to the war had never been of great service, and had always gone into difficulties with the Russian officers. Their complaints were loud and frequent, and in 1705, when the two Cossack regiments were with the Russian troops near Grodno, Mazepa received a long letter from Gorlenko, their commander, complaining of the rudeness and insults of the Russians, and of an order that was said to be issued sending the Cossack regiments to Prussia to study the art of war and to be turned into regular dragoons. On reading this letter, Mazepa, in a fit of natural indignation, said to his trusty secretary, Orlik: 'What good can we hope for in return for our faithful services? Another man in my place would not have been such a fool as to have refused the offers of Stanislas.' Not long after this Mazepa accepted an invitation from Prince Wisniowiecki to be godfather to his daughter. There he met and became intimate with the Princess Dolska, the mother of his host. The confidential conversations at the christening—conversations from which politics were not excluded—brought about a correspondence in cipher. In some of the letters of the Princess there were allusions of such a nature that Mazepa found it necessary to explain them to Orlik. When in one letter she urged him to begin what he intended, and assured him that all his wishes would be granted, and that he would soon have the support of the whole Swedish army, Mazepa affected great indignation at the idea of an old woman thinking she could snare such 'a wily old bird' as he was, and exclaimed at the folly it would be for him under the present circumstances to abandon the living for the sake of the dead, and leave one shore without being able to reach the other. He ordered Orlik to reply: 'I beg you to stop this correspondence, which can ruin me in life, honor, and substance. Do not hope or imagine that in my old age I can act disloyally to the Tsar.' For a long time there were no letters, but finally the Princess spread a snare which caught the 'wily old bird'. She wrote from Lemberg that she had been at another christening, and had sat at dinner between Sheremetief and Ronne, who had let her understand that

Menshikof was digging a pit for him, in order to be elected Hetman in his stead. At this Mazepa lost control of himself, and began to recount all the indignities which he and the Cossacks had suffered since the war began, and especially his personal difficulties with Menshikof, and the hints he had so often had that the Russians intended to turn the Ukraine into a regular Russian province, and try to satisfy him with the title of Prince. He answered the Princess, with thanks for her friendship and her warning. While at Kiev in 1707, Mazepa received another letter from King Stanislas, enclosed in one from his friend. He was startled, and let it fall from his hands, and exclaiming, 'Oh, cursed old woman, you will ruin me!' sat for along while in deep thought. Then turning to Orlik, he said: 'I am struggling in my mind whether to send this letter to the Tsar or not. Let us advise about it tomorrow, and meanwhile you go home and pray to God. Perhaps your prayers will avail more than mine, because you live in more Christian ways. God knows that I am doing nothing for myself, but only for all of you and your wives and children.' Going home and getting some money, though it was late at night, Orlik went to the monasteries and distributed alms to the monks, nuns, and poor people who were sleeping in the outbuildings. He got at first nothing but curses for his kindness; they took him for a thief. When Orlik returned the next morning Mazepa was holding in his hand a bit of the true Cross, and exclaimed: 'I protest before the all-seeing God that not for my private profit, nor for higher honors, nor for greater riches, nor for any other aims of mine, but for all of you, your wives and children, for the general good of our poor mother country the Ukraine, of the Zaporovian army and of the Ukrainian people, and for the increase and extension of the rights and liberties of the army, I wish by the aid of God to act so that you shall not be ruined either by Moscow or by Sweden.' Then kissing the Cross, he swore Orlik to secrecy, and dictated an answer to Stanislas, giving various reasons why he could not obey his commands, but promising at the same time to do nothing which would be harmful to his interests or to those of the Swedes.

CHAPTER 62

MAZEPA'S SECRET PLAN FOR UKRAINIAN INDEPENDENCE

Mazepa's plan had been to preserve as far as possible his neutrality, making excuses for not taking actively the part of the Russians, and not espousing the side of the Swedes, until he saw that Charles was sure to win. He had reckoned that Swedish invasion would be turned towards the north and towards Moscow. Now, when he discovered that the march of Charles was towards the Ukraine, his combinations were all disturbed. He must take sides either with the Russians or the Swedes, and in any case there was a danger that the Ukraine would be the battle-field, and that the Cossacks would be ground to pieces between the millstones. On ascertaining the movements of the Swedes, Peter had ordered Mazepa to send a force of Cossacks to fall on the rear of the Swedes, and suggested that it would be well for their Hetman to take command of this force in person. Mazepa excused himself on the ground of his gout and frightful pains which prevented him from riding. He was very successful in feigning illness, and not unfrequently, for reasons of his own, covered himself with plasters and passed whole days in bed. The belief in his feeble health made his rivals prefer waiting to plotting. At the same time he informed the Tsar of the immediate danger which might arise if he left the country, as it was in the most unsettled condition. There was no one he could leave behind of whom he felt sure. As Peter feared the effect in the Ukraine of the Swedish proclamations, he allowed Mazepa to stay at home; but after the battle of Liesna, when the Swedes were already near the Ukrainian frontier, he asked him to come to a conference in the town of Starodub, and, to his answers about the difficulties he expected with the Cossacks, told him to appoint some one to take his place and come without fail. Mazepa called together four Cossack colonels who had already on several occasions complained to him of the Russians, expressed their fears of what might happen if they came into the country, and begged him to think of the general safety. He asked them whether he should go to Starodub. 'Do not go,' said Lomikofsky, 'otherwise you will ruin yourself and us and all the Ukraine. We have already so many times begged you to send to Charles, but you have always delayed, and have literally slept. Here now are the Russians coming into the country,—to the ruin and death of us all, and the Swedes are here too!" Mazepa upbraided them, threatened to leave them to their fate and go himself to the Tsar, but finally grew milder, and asked 'Shall I send to the King or not?' 'Send by all means; it was time long ago,' they replied. Mazepa then ordered Orlik to write a letter in Latin to Count Piper, in which he declared his joy at the arrival of the Swedes, begged for assistance to free the whole of the Ukraine from the heavy Muscovite yoke, and promised to prepare a ferry across the Desna. At the same time he sent his nephew, Voinarofsky, to Menshikof to say that he was almost at the point of death, and was going from Baturin to Borzna to receive extreme unction from the Archbishop of Kiev. 'This news has made me very sad,' wrote Menshikof to the Tsar; 'first, because I have not succeeded in seeing him, which it is very necessary for me to do; and secondly, because I am sorry for such a good man if God does not relieve him from his disease. With regard to that, he writes that his gout has brought on an attack of epilepsy.' Menshikof resolved to go to Borzna and see the Hetman on his sick bed. At nearly the same time Mazepa received a message that the Swedes would be the next day on the Desna, and Voinarofsky, who had left Mazepa's camp in the night, arrived to say that Menshikof had resolved to see him at all hazards. Without waiting for Menshikof, Mazepa left Borzna, and arrived late at night at Baturin. Having given orders to defend that town, he set out the next day with the Cossack chiefs, many officers, and an escort of 1,500 men, straight for the Swedish camp. On arriving there, he took an oath with his followers that he accepted the Swedish protection, not for any private profit of his own, but for the good of his fatherland and of the Cossacks.

On his way to Borzna, Menshikof heard that Mazepa had gone to Baturin, and turned towards that town, but was refused admittance. This made him suspect something wrong, and his suspicions were confirmed when he heard that Mazepa had crossed the Desna. Soon some Cossack officers came to his camp to ask for protection against the Hetman, who had gone over to the enemy.

CHAPTER 63

CZAR PETER'S PLAN AGAINST MAZEPA

Peter was with the main army on the Desna watching the movements of the enemy, when, on November 7, he received Menshikof's letter announcing the treason of Mazepa. He answered it the same night, ordering him to take precautionary measures against the spread of the rebellious spirit, to prevent the Cossacks from joining the enemy, and to keep on good terms with the colonels and other leaders of the Cossacks, and to persuade them to elect a new Hetman. The next day he issued a manifesto to the Ukrainians announcing that Mazepa had treacherously deserted to the Swedes, 'in order to put the land of the Ukraine as before under the dominion of Poland, and to turn over the churches and the monasteries to the Uniates.' To Apraxin, who had just informed him of his victory over Lybecker, he wrote: 'Although it is against my conscience to write anything bad to you in return for your good news, yet necessity compels me to tell you that Mazepa has turned out a new Judas, for, after being loyal to me for twenty-one years, now, when he is almost in his coffin, he has become a traitor and betrayer of his people. Indeed, although this is bad business, yet he did not do it with the approval of all, but only with five persons, and the people here, after hearing of it, complained of him with tears to God, and are indescribably bitter against him, since, as we hear, his life was apart from God. Therefore we hope in God that he has done more harm to himself than to him whom he intended to injure.'

It was decided in a council of war to attack Baturin, the Cossack capital, before Mazepa and the Swedes should have time to reach it. Menshikof, who had come to Peter's camp for conference with him, hastened to Baturin, where Prince Dimitri Golitsyn was waiting. The Cossacks refused to allow the Russians to enter before the new Hetman was elected, and tried to prevent them from crossing the river. That night the garrison sent word to Menshikof that they were faithful to the Tsar, and would allow his troops to enter, but demanded three days for their free exit. Menshikof replied the next morning, refusing to give them the time demanded, but telling them to come out at once without fear and no one would harm them. They at first wished to kill the messenger, but finally let him go with the cry, 'We will all die here, but we will not let the Tsar's troops come in.' Early the next morning (November 13) Menshikof ordered the assault, and in two hours the town, which was badly fortified, was taken. No one was spared except the leaders, who were reserved for punishment. The arms were kept for the Government, but all the property of the inhabitants was given up to the soldiery. The whole town, including the stores so necessary to the Swedes, was burnt to the ground. Baturin as a stronghold ceased to exist. It is now but a village.

CHAPTER 64

MAZEPA DENOUNCED AS HETMAN

The ruin of Baturin had a very salutary effect upon the discontented spirits among the Cossacks. It entirely baffled the plans of Mazepa. On the very day when the Swedes crossed the Desna, Peter went quietly to Glukhof, where the metropolitan of Kief, two archbishops, the four colonels who had remained faithful, and the leaders of the Cossacks were assembled. An election was held according to the consecrated usage, and Skoropadsky, the Colonel of Starodub, on the wish of Peter, was chosen Hetman. On the same day, November 18, Mazepa was publicly excommunicated and cursed. To impress this more on the minds of the Cossacks, his portrait was taken into the church, the blue ribbon of St. Andrew was taken from it, and it was then dragged through the streets and hung on the gallows, after which the traitors captured at Baturin were executed. The ceremony of the anathema of Mazepa was repeated at Moscow a few days afterwards, and his name was formally added to that of the false Dimitri, Stenka Razin, and others in the comminatory service read in the Russian churches in the first week of Lent. This ceremony took place until 1869, when the names of Dimitri and Mazepa were dropped. The proclamation announcing Mazepa's excommunication, and threatening other traitors with the same fate, was affixed to the doors of all the churches in Little Russia.

Of those who had gone over with Mazepa to the Swedes, Colonel Danilo Apostol and Colonel Galagan soon abandoned him and were pardoned by the Russians. Apostol brought a verbal message purporting to be from Mazepa, that he would deliver up 'the chief personage' into Russian hands if he were assured of pardon and of being restored to his position as Hetman, under the guarantee of foreign Powers. A favorable answer was returned, but nothing further was heard from Mazepa. Later on other Cossacks deserted from the Swedish camp, until Mazepa was almost the only one left. The Swedes therefore profited little by his adherence.

Peter issued a manifesto inviting the Zaporovian Cossacks to obey the orders of the new Hetman Skoropadsky, and both sides distributed proclamations throughout the Ukraine in order to quiet or rouse the population. Charles, on his side, declaimed against the heavy Muscovite yoke: Peter replied with accounts of the maltreatment of the Cossack prisoners by the Swedes, of the insults offered to orthodox churches, and of the intention to compel the Cossacks to embrace the Lutheran and Uniate religions. Charles then talked about the Russian attacks on the liberties of the Ukraine, and spoke of negotiations of Peter with the Pope, the permission given to the Jesuits to have schools and churches in Russia, and of the Tsar's purpose to become a Catholic after the war. Peter invited the Ukrainians to put all sorts of obstacles in the way of the enemy, to leave him without roof, food, or fire, and offered a reward of 2,000 rubles for every general taken prisoner, of 1,000 rubles for every colonel, proportionately for the other officers, of five rubles for every common soldier, and of three rubles for every dead body brought in. The mainfestoes of Charles and the 'universals' of the fallen and anathematised Hetman had little or no effect. The peasants hid their property and their grain, captured the Swedes wherever they could, and drove off their horses. Peter wrote to Apraxin: 'The people of the Ukraine stand, with God's help, more firmly than was possible to expect. The King sends enticing proclamations, but the people remain faithful and bring in the King's letters.'

CHAPTER 65

MAZEPA'S DEATH
THE RUSSIAN VERSION

Mazepa died at Varnitza, a village near Bender on March 31, 1710 and was buried in the Old Church of St. George on the high bank of the Danube at Galatz and transferred in the mid-1800's to the Church of the Virgin there.

From the works of Eugene Schuyler, Phd.;
author of Turkistan and Peter the Great, published in 1884

CHAPTER 66

KAZAK: ORIGIN OF THE WORD COSSACK

The Peoples of Western Siberia In the 15th Century

The Tatars living east of the Urals along the Tobol River formed a separate Siberian khanate. In the 16th century the city situated at the mouth of the Tobol, which the Russians called "Siberia", became it's capital. The Siberian khanate was not a united kingdom. It was broken up into a large number of small principalities (ulusi) whose petty princes enjoyed a large measure of independence.

The Siberian Tatars engaged in cattle raising and to some extent in agriculture, but the chief wealth of their land lay in their valuable fur-bearing animals (sable, marten, beaver, squirrel, etc.). Hunting provided the Siberian Tatars with a profitable article of exchange with the more cultured lands of Asia (Bokhara and Khiva.) The Siberian Tatars also obtained furs by robbing their neighbors, the trappers, from whom they collected tribute in furs.

Along the upper reaches of the Tura and to the north of it lived the Mansi (Voguls); along the lower reaches of the Irtysh and along the Ob—the Khanti (Ostiaks). Both of these peoples were divided into small tribes ruled by petty princes. The Mansi lived by hunting. Each clan owned a section of forest where it set up enclosures for the catching of elk and placed arbalests. Some of the Mansi practiced a rudimentary form of agriculture and cattle breeding. The Khanti lived chiefly by fishing. Those of the tribe who inhabited the tundra raised herds of northern elk.

The Mansi and the Khanti were heathens: the Khanti worshipped the bear, which they regarded as their ancestor. Whenever they killed a bear they performed a sacred song and dance over it, to "atone for their sin".

The Tatars conquered the Mansi and the Khanti and forced them to pay tribute in furs. In case of war the Vogul and Ostiak princelings had to go with their troops to help the Tatars.

To the north of the Khanti the Nentsi (Samoyedes) roamed the tundra with their herds of elk. In the spring they moved on to the Ob River for fishing. The vast tundra made the Nentsi inaccessible to the conquerors; they therefore did not fall under the rule of the Tatars.

In the middle of the 15th century the Kazakh khanate was formed east of the Urals, on the land of present-day Kazakhstan. The nomadic peoples comprising it had formerly belonged to a union of Uzbek tribes. In 1456, they separated from the Uzbeks and formed an independent kingdom. The Kazakhs received their name from the fact that they had separated from the Uzbeks (the word kazakh in Turkic means "a free man who has broken away from his tribe", from which comes the Russian word kazak— Cossack + Cosack meaning "a free man").

CHAPTER 67

MAZEPA'S FALL FROM GRACE
WITH PETER THE GREAT

In the meantime the war with Sweden went on. Many campaigns were fought, for the contest was continued through several successive years. The King of Sweden made repeated attempts to destroy the new city of St. Petersburg, but without success. On the contrary, the town grew and prospered more and more; and the shelter and protection which the fortifications around it afforded to the mouth of the river and to the adjacent roadsteads enabled the Czar to go on so rapidly in building new ships, and in thus increasing and strengthening his fleet, that very soon he was much stronger than the King of Sweden in all the neighboring waters, so that he not only was able to keep the enemy very effectually at bay, but he even made several successful descents upon the Swedish territory along the adjoining coasts.

But, while the Czar was thus rapidly increasing his power at sea, the King of Sweden proved himself the strongest on land. He extended his conquests very rapidly in Poland and in the adjoining provinces, and at last, in the summer of 1708, he conceived the design of crossing the Dnieper and threatening Moscow, which was still Peter's capital. He accordingly pushed his forces forward until he approached the bank of the river. He came up to it at a certain point, as if he was intending to cross there. Peter assembled all his troops on the opposite side of the river at that point in order to oppose him. But the demonstration which the king made of an intention to cross at that point was only a pretense. He left a sufficient number of men there to make a show, and secretly marched away the great body of his troops in the night to a point about three miles farther up the river, where he succeeded in crossing with them before the emperor's forces had any suspicion strong enough to oppose him in the open field, were obliged immediately to retreat, and leave him in full possession of the ground.

Peter was now much alarmed. He sent an officer to the camp of the King of Sweden with a flag of truce, to ask on what terms the king would make peace with him. But Charles was too much elated with his success in crossing the river and placing himself in a position from which he could advance, without encountering any farther obstruction, to the very gates of the capital, to be willing then to propose any terms. So he declined entering into any negotiation, saying only in a haughty tone "that he would treat with his brother Peter at Moscow".

On mature reflection, however, he seems to have concluded that it would be more prudent for him not to march at once to Moscow, and so he turned his course for a time toward the southward, in the direction of the Crimea and the Black Sea.

CHAPTER 68

CHARLES XII'S SECRETS WITH MAZEPA

There was one secret reason which induced the King of Sweden to move thus to the southward which Peter did not for a time understand. The country of the Cossacks lay in that direction, and the famous Mazepa, of whom some account has already been given in this volume, was the chieftain of the Cossacks, and he, as it happened, had had a quarrel with the Czar, and in consequence of it had opened a secret negotiation with the King of Sweden, and had agreed that if the king would come into his part of the country he would desert the cause of the Czar, and would come over to his side, with all the Cossacks under his command.

The cause of Mazepa's quarrel with the Czar was this: He was one day paying a visit to his majesty, and, while seated at table, Peter began to complain of the lawless and ungovernable character of the Cossacks, and to propose that Mazepa should introduce certain reforms in the organization and discipline of the tribe, with a view of bringing them under more effectual control. It is probable that the reforms which he proposed were somewhat analogous to those which he had introduced so successfully into the armies under his own more immediate command.

Mazepa opposed this suggestion. He said that the attempt to adopt such measures with the Cossacks would never succeed; that the men were so wild and savage by nature, and so fixed in the rude and irregular habits of warfare to which they and their fathers have been so long accustomed, that they could never be made to submit to such restrictions as a regular military discipline would impose.

Peter, who never could endure the least opposition or contradiction to any of his ideas or plans, became quite angry with Mazepa on account of the objections which he made to his proposals, and, as was usual with him in such cases, he broke out in the most rude and violent language imaginable. He called Mazepa an enemy and a traitor, and threatened to have him impaled alive. It is true he did not really mean what he said, his words being only empty threats dictated by the brutal violence of his anger. Still, Mazepa was very much offended. He went away from the Czar's tent muttering his displeasure, and resolving secretly on revenge.

Soon after this Mazepa opened the communication above referred to with the King of Sweden, and at last an agreement was made between them by which it was stipulated that the king was to advance into the southern part of the country, where, of course, the Cossacks would be sent out to meet him, and then Mazepa was to revolt from the Czar, and go over with all his forces to the King of Sweden's side. By this means the Czar's army was sure, they thought, to be defeated; and in this case the King of Sweden was to remain in possession of the Russian territory, while the Cossacks were to retire to their own fortresses, and live thenceforth as an independent tribe.

CHAPTER 69

THE PLOT OF MAZEPA

The plot seemed to be very well laid; but, unfortunately for the contrivers of it, it was not destined to succeed. In the first place, Mazepa's scheme of revolting with the Cossacks to the enemy was discovered by the Czar, and almost entirely defeated, before the time arrived for putting it into execution. Peter had his secret agents every where, and through them he received such information in respect to Mazepa's movements as led him to suspect his designs. He said nothing, however, but manoeuvred his forces so as to have a large body of troops that he could rely upon always near Mazepa and the Cossacks, and between them and the army of the Swedes. He ordered the officers of these troops to watch Mazepa's movements closely, and to be ready to act against him at a moment's notice, should occasion require. Mazepa was somewhat disconcerted in his plans by this state of things; but he could not make any objection, for the troops thus stationed near him seemed to be placed there for the purpose of cooperating with him against the enemy.

CHAPTER 70

MAZEPA'S PLAN

In the mean time, Mazepa cautiously made known his plans to the leading men among the Cossacks as fast as he thought it prudent to do so. He represented to them how much better it would be for them to be restored to their former liberty as an independent tribe, instead of being in subjugation to such a despot as the Czar. He also enumerated the various grievances which they suffered under Russian rule, and endeavored to excite the animosity of his bearers as much as possible against Peter's government.

He found that the chief officers of the Cossacks seemed quite disposed to listen to what he said, and to adopt his views. Some of them were really so, and others pretended to be so for fear of displeasing him. At length he thought it time to take some measures for preparing the minds of the men generally for what was to come, and in order to do this he determined on publicly sending a messenger to the Czar with the complaints which he had to make in behalf of his men. The men, knowing of this embassy, and understanding the grounds of the complaint which Mazepa was to make by means of it, would be placed, he thought, in such a position that, in the event of an unfavorable answer being returned, as he had no doubt would be the case, they could be the more easily led into the revolt which he proposed.

CHAPTER 71

MAZEPA'S NEPHEW

Mazepa accordingly made out a statement of his complaints, and appointed his nephew a commissioner to proceed to head-quarters and lay them before the Czar. The name of the nephew was Warnarowski. As soon as Warnarowski arrived at the camp, Peter, instead of granting him an audience, and listening to the statement which he had to make, ordered him to be seized and sent to prison, as if he were guilty of a species of treason in coming to trouble his sovereign with complaints and difficulties at such a time, when the country was suffering under an acutal invasion from a foreign enemy.

As soon as Mazepa heard that his nephew was arrested, he was convinced that his plots had been discovered,and that he must not lose a moment in carrying them into execution, or all would be lost. He accordingly immediately put his whole force in motion to march toward the place where the Swedish army was then posted,

94

ostensibly for the purpose of attacking them. He crossed a certain river which lay between him and the Swedes, and then, when safely over, he stated to his men what he intended to do.

The men were filled with indignation at this proposal, which, being wholly unexpected, came upon them by surprise. They refused to join in the revolt. A scene of great excitement and confusion followed. A portion of the Cossacks, those with whom Mazepa had come to an understanding beforehand, were disposed to go with him, but the rest were filled with vexation and rage. They declared that they would seize their chieftain, bind him hand and foot, and send him to the Czar. Indeed, it is highly probable that the two factions would have come soon to a bloody fight for the possession of the person of their chieftain, in which case he would very likely have been torn to pieces in the struggle, if those who were disposed to revolt had not fled before the opposition to their movement had time to become organized. Mazepa and those who adhered to him—about two thousand men in all—went over in a body to the camp of the Swedes. The rest, led by the officers that still remained faithful, marched at once to the nearest body of Russian forces, and put themselves under the command of the Russian general there.

CHAPTER 72

COUNCIL OF WAR

A council of war was soon after called in the Russian camp for the purpose of bringing Mazepa to trial. He was, of course, found guilty, and sentence of death—with a great many indignities to accompany the execution—was passed upon him. The sentence, however, could not be executed upon Mazepa himself, for he was out of the reach of his accusers, being safe in the Swedish camp. So they made a wooden image or effigy to represent him, and inflicted the penalties upon the substitute instead.

In the first place, they dressed the effigy to imitate the appearance of Mazepa, and put upon it representations of the medals, ribbons, and other decorations which he was accustomed to wear. They brought this figure out before the camp, in presence of the general and of all the leading officers, the soldiers being also drawn up around the spot. A herald appeared and read the sentence of condemnation, and then proceeded to carry it into execution, as follows. First, he tore Mazepa's patent of knighthood in pieces, and threw the fragments into the air. Then he tore off the medals and decorations from the image, and, throwing them upon the ground, he trampled them under his feet. Then he struck the effigy itself a blow by which it was overturned and left prostrate in the dust.

The hangman then came up, and, tying a halter round the neck of the effigy, dragged it of to a place where a gibbet had been erected, and hanged it there.

Immediately after this ceremony, the Cossacks, according to their custom, proceeded to elect a new chieftain in the place of Mazepa. The chieftain thus chosen came forward before the Czar to take the oath of allegiance to him, and to offer him his homage.

From the works of Jacob Abbott; author of Peter the Great, published 1859.

CHAPTER 73

VIEWS OF SWEDEN

I, Dr. S. C. Mazepa, would like to present two different viewpoints of the demise of Mazepa. One, being the Swedish King Charles XII's view. The other, Peter the Great's; Czar of Russia, viewpoint. Each chapter will conflict each other's view and I, Dr. S. C. Mazepa, would like the reader to choose the desired version of Mazepa's end.

KING CHARLES XII of SWEDEN

When Charles XII of Sweden turned southwards in the direction of Severia and the Ukraine he hoped to find a serviceable ally in Mazepa, the Hetman of the Ukrainian Cossacks. As the connection of this man with the Swedish King has been much misunderstood, and his influence on the events of 1708-1709 greatly exaggerated, it is necessary to briefly explain who he was and what he really did.

Ivan Stefanovich Mazepa, whom art and poetry have conspired to make one of the most picturesque figures in Slavonic history, his name from the castle of Mazepa near Bialozerkiew the place of his birth. In his youth he served as a page at the Court of King John Casimir, but, being caught with the wife of a Polish magnate, was tarred and feathered, bound naked on the back of his own horse with his face to it's tail and his legs tied beneath it's belly and let loose upon the steppes of the Ukraine. Here he was rescued from the carrion crows by the Cossacks who adopted the lad. He grew up among them, and in 1687, they unanimously elected him their Hetman. In this position he greatly distinguished himself by his valour and capacity, clearing the land of the Tartar hordes, and rendering signal services to Peter the Great during his earlier Turkish wars. But it was the secret ambition of Mazepa to become independent of both Russia and Poland, and the successes of Charles XII seemed to present him with his long sought for opportunity. During Charles' march through Poland in 1708, Mazepa, who had long been vacillating between loyalty and rebellion, began secretly negotiating with the Swedes through King Stanislaus. For the Cossack Hetman, although bound by all the ties of honor and gratitude to the Tsar, had been much disturbed by Peter's far-reaching military reforms which seemed to him to be undermining the independence of the Cossacks, and he was quite prepared to shake off the Muscovite yoke, if only he had a powerful friend behind him. Such a friend he now hoped to find in Charles XII, and the reward he claimed for his defection was the erection of a principality for himself consisting of the Ukraine and a couple of adjacent Polish palatinates, yet all the time he adroitly hoodwinked Peter by pretending to reveal to him the secret plans of Charles and Stanislaus. It was while Charles was resting at Mohilev, after the battle of Holowczyn, that Mazepa took the decisive step by sending a special envoy to the Swedish monarch, offering to place 30,000 horsemen at his disposal, if he would take the Cossacks of the Ukraine under his protection. Charles consented. Hitherto indeed the possibility of Mazepa's active assistance seems scarcely to have entered into his calculations, and he received all the Cossack Hetman's earlier overtures with the most frigid indifference. It was not in Charles' nature to willingly seek help from anyone, and the monarch who had rejected the offer of 20,000 picked troops from Prussia, on practically his own terms, was not likely to attach too much importance to the promises of a discontented freebooter in the Russian steppes. It was only when necessity compelled him to abandon for a time the advance on Moscow, that he gave a thought to Mazepa, though the knowledge that he actually possessed an ally in the Ukraine was an additional argument for turning in that direction now that there was nothing better to do, or hope for. The wish moreover to join Mazepa as soon as possible was his chief reason for not awaiting, and so sacrificing, Levenhaupt and the valuable caravan of stores and provisions which that unfortunate general was now painfully endeavouring to bring with him all the way from the Gulf of Riga to the banks of the Dnieper, a distance of more than four hundred miles.

In fact, Charles had laid upon the shoulders of his lieutenant a burden too heavy for him to bear. On May 26, the King had sent Levenhaupt a command to set out from Riga at the beginning of

June, march straight to the Dnieper, and there await further orders. This letter did not reach Levenhaupt till June 8th and he at once replied that with the best will in the world it was impossible for him to get all his baggage wagons together till the end of the month. By that time he was ready, and set out with 11,000 men, and sufficient provisions to feed the main army for twelve weeks. It is said that each company took with it ten four-horse wagons. Hampered as he was by these impediments, Levenhaupt's progress was necessarily slow, and it was made slower still by the bad roads and the heavy rains, so that it was not till the middle of September that he reached the Dnieper at Sklow where fresh orders bade him follow southwards after the main army as best he could, along and across the rivers Dnieper and Sosz, to Starodub in Severia, some hundred and fifty miles farther on. Levenhaupt, who had expected to find the King waiting for him on the Dnieper, was thunderstruck at thus being abandoned by the main army from which he was now separated by no less than five large rivers, and his dismay was not diminished when he learned that the Tsar was marching rapidly towards him, with a threefold odds, to surround and cut him off. He felt that he was indeed in evil case, but he prepared, like the brave man he was, to loyally carry out the King's orders and his strategy at this crisis was not unworthy of his great reputation. Within a week he had crossed the Dnieper, and, fighting incessantly with the Russian vanguard, forced his way towards the Sosz, but, when only a day's march from that river at Lesna, Peter threw himself in the way with 30,000 men, and Levenhaupt and his 8,000 had nothing for it but to conquer or die. Early on September 29, the battle began, and lasted till dusk, the Swedes gallantly repulsing four determined attacks. The same night the Russians received large reinforcements, 15,000 men, so that Levenhaupt thought it prudent to quit his camp, and make for the Sosz which he hoped to cross at Propoisk before he was overtaken. But the Russians followed hard upon him; part of his army missed it's way, and was lost; the passage of the Sosz at Propoisk proved impracticable; so Levenhaupt, after sinking his cannon in the morasses and burning the whole of his stores and ammunition, to prevent them from falling into the enemy's hands, retreated with barely 6,000 men, and succeeded, after incredible hardships, in reaching Severia.

CHAPTER 74

PETER EXULTS OVER MAZEPA

Well might Peter the Great exult over the victory of Lesna, and consider it cheaply bought even at the cost of 6,000 men. To say nothing of the very serious material damage inflicted on the Swedes by the total loss of indispensable stores and ammunition, it was the first time they had been defeated in a pitched battle by the Russians, and the moral effect of such a reversal of the usual course of things was incalculable. Not without reason did the Tsar call the battle of Lesna "the mother of Pultava".

Charles received the tidings of this disaster with his usual sangfroid, nay more, having regard to the fact that the larger portion of Levenhaupt's army had got off, he chose to regard it as "a lucky action". He himself, meanwhile, was continuing his march through Severia. Severia was the name then given to the plain lying between the rivers Desna and Sosz, corresponding almost exactly with the modern government of Chernigov. It consists, for the most part, of forest and morass, which made progress, especially for the baggage, very slow and difficult. The country here was not wasted like the Dnieper district, and in some places a little forage could be scraped together, but the Swedes found all the villages they came to deserted, while in the towns (which were few and far between) the inhabitants suspiciously watched the invaders from behind their walls, armed to the teeth. Food became scarcer and scarcer as the march proceeded, even the more squeamish of the officers being now glad enough to live upon black bread and tisane. In the beginning of October, Levenhaupt affected his junction with his master, but both armies had now shrunk so much from their former proportions, that the King ordered the newcomers to be incorporated with his own regiments, and thus many officers, including Levenhaupt himself, had no longer any command. Shortly after this junction, when Charles reached the little Severian town of Horki, he was joined (November 6th) by Mazepa who came with all the ceremony of a Hetman of Cossacks, having the silver staff borne before the horse-tail standard behind him, but bringing with him only 1,500 horsemen instead of the 30,000 he had promised.

CHAPTER 75

MAZEPA'S GAMBLE

Mazepa, in fact, had lost nearly everything, and was now himself a fugitive. He had for long succeeded in hoodwinking the Tsar, but his double dealing had at last come to light, and Peter took prompt measures to make his rebellious vassal a useless ally to anyone else. Menshikov, with a large Russian army, suddenly appeared in the Ukraine, reduced Baturin, Mazepa's capital, to ashes (previously confiscating the treasure accumulated there estimated at 2,000,000 gulden);placed Russian garrisons in the fortresses of Starodub and Novgorod Seversk; caused Mazepa to be publicly excommunicated by the Archbishop of Liev, and made his former lieutenant, Skoropadzki, though he was no longer a potent ally, his sagacity, courage and intimate knowledge of the country made him a valuable counsellor and guide. He also lent Charles a large sum of ready money. Charles seems to have been very favorably impressed by the wit and vivacity of the wiry little man who, despite his sixty years, was still full of fire and energy, and spoke Latin as fluently as the King himself. Ten days after meeting Mazepa, Charles reached (November 15th) the broad and rapid Desna which separates Severia from the Ukraine. The Russians had assembled in large numbers on the opposite bank, and the banks on the Swedish side were so steep that the soldiers had to be hoisted down on to the rafts prepared for them; but the passage was nevertheless safely effected, and, after a sever skirmish, the enemy was put to flight. And now, at last, Charles found himself in the Ukraine.

The Ukraine, the "border-land" (Hence the name. Beyond it lay the land of the Tartars, stretching north-eastwards as far as the China) in those days between Europe and Tartary, nominally belonging to Russia and Poland, but actually in the possession of the Cossacks, was the name given to that district which extended on both sides of the lower Dnieper, south of the city of Kiev. It was a fat and fruitful land abounding in cereals and rich grasses, and covered with flocks and herds, and here the Swedes were much better off than they had been for some time, although they had come to it at the wrong time, and were now as good as cut off altogether from the rest of the world. After marching past the smoking ruins of Mazepa's former stronghold, Baturin, Charles fixed his head-quarters at Romny, a little place to the south-east of it, situated on the River Sula. Throughout his march, he was harassed incessantly by the light horse of the Russians, whose main army now lay towards the north, with it's foreposts extending as far as Lebedin and Veprik. It was from Romny that Charles issued a manifesto (written in excellent Latin by his field secretary Hermelin) to the Cossacks, warning them against Peter's treachery, and offering to take them under his protection; but it produced far less effect than a previous proclamation by the Tsar, appealing to the cupidity of the freebooters by offering rewards on a graduated scale (two thousand rubels were to be paid for every general, 1,000 for every colonel, down to 5 rubels for every live, and 3 rubels for every dead, common soldier. In many places, moreover, circulars were left behind, promising the Swedish soldiers plenty of good food and handsome pay if they would desert), for every Swedish captive brought into the Russian camp, alive or dead. All this time the Swedes had little or no rest. The Russian armies, reinforced by thousands of Cossacks, were closing in upon them on every side, rendering it more and more difficult every day to collect supplies. At length Romny became too narrow for them, and in December they shifted their quarters to Hadyach, still farther to the south-east.

CHAPTER 76

MAZEPA'S DEEP FREEZE

It was while the ragged, half-starved army was making it's way towards this place that a terrible frost, the like of which had not been known for a century, devastated all Europe. In Sweden and Norway elks and harts were found frozen to death in the forests. The Baltic became a mass of ice. In Central Europe the fruit trees were killed by the thousands, the canals of Venice, the estuary of the Tagus, even the swift-flowing Rhine, were covered with ice. But it was in the vast open steppes of the Ukraine that the cold was most severe. There birds dropped down dead from the trees and wine and spirits froze into solid masses of ice. It was while the unhappy Swedes were painfully toiling on their way between Romny and Hadyach that this new and terrible enemy fell upon them. They hastened as rapidly as they could to Hadyach for warmth and shelter, but on reaching the place it was found that there was only a single gate through which they could enter, and that was speedily blocked by wagons and cannon, horses and men. Only a fraction of the army could get inside the town that same evening, the rest had to pass three or four nights among the snow-drifts under the open sky, and the consequence was a loss of life greater than the carnage of a pitched battle. Three to four thousand men were frozen to death, and of the remainder there was scarcely one who was not seriously injured by frost-bite. Even those who lay well covered with sheepskins in beds of straw were afraid of falling asleep lest they should freeze to death and many had not even skins to protect them. It was no unusual thing to find a sentinel frozen to death on horseback, and sledges full of corpses were driven every day into the little town, every house of which now became a veritable hospital, the patients being crowded together on benches and under benches, so that there was no room to move about. The sufferings of the unhappy wretches were aggravated by ignorance or recklessness. Many thought it absurd to rub their frozen limbs with snow, the only sure remedy; others tried to drown their woes in bad brandy and crude Tartar wine, while others again were too weak and helpless to attempt to do anything for themselves. "Nevertheless," grimly exclaims the young Duke of Wurtemberg, a participator in these horrors, "nevertheless, although Earth, Sky and Air were now against us, the King's designs had to be accomplished, and the daily march to be made." Charles himself in his letter to his sister Ulrica, some months later, passes lightly enough over the intense sufferings of his soldiers, and evidently thinks it a sufficient compensation that they were able now and then to have some lively skirmishes by way of diversion; but, though a long experience of war had had the natural effect of making him somewhat callous, there is no reason to exclaim against him as altogether heartless. A thorough soldier himself, he naturally regarded warfare entirely from a warrior's point of view. He knew that the profession of arms was as grim as it was glorious; but he argued, not unreasonably, that a man enters it with his eyes open, and that a true soldier is in duty bound to cheerfully take the rough with the smooth in the trade of his own choosing. He himself in this respect always set the example. Throughout the awful winter of 1708-1709, he took more than his fair share of fatigue and hardship with perfect equanimity, exacting nothing from his soldiers that he did not cheerfully undergo himself, and it is a fact that his soldiers regarded him more as a comrade than as a master. Then, too, as a prudent general ought to do, he minimised difficulties as much as possible, making light of what could not be altered or denied. On one occasion he was accosted by a soldier who held out to him a piece of black bread almost as hard as a stone, exclaiming: "That, your Majesty, is what we have to eat"! Charles at once took the bread, broke off a bit, chewed and swallowed it, and then said: "It is not very good to eat, my lad, but it can be eaten." On another occasion he was riding by an ambulance wagon in which lay young ensign, a relative of Count Piper, who had lost both feet at Hadjach from frost-bite. Charles stopped and asked him how he was. The youth replied that he would never be able to walk again as the greater part of his heels and toes was gone. "Stuff! Stuff!" replied the King, then baring his own leg up to the ankle, he added: "I have seen fellows who have lost their legs up to there, yet when they stuffed them into their jackboots, they have managed to walk all right". On riding away, however, he said in an undertone to his adjutant: "I'm sorry for him though, poor fellow! he is so very young". Such anecdotes have sometimes been given as instances of the young King's (he was only 26 at the time) hard-heartedness. I prefer to see in them a rough perhaps, but certainly kind intention to make the best of things, and it is a fact that so long as he was able to mingle with his men, and lead them personally, they endured their torments without a murmur.

CHAPTER 77

CHARLES' OFFENSIVE

All this time Charles was consumed by a restless energy which was rewarded by several successes. Early in January, 1709, the little fortress of Veprik surrendered to the Swedes though not till after they had lost 1,000 men beneath it's walls. At the end of

February Charles suddenly assumed the offensive, and defeated the enemy in two very sharp engagements at Oposznaya and Krasnokutsk, on the latter occasion driving ten thousand Russians headlong before him. Then the spring floods put an end to all active operations for a time; the Tsar set off for Voronets on the Don, to inspect his Black Sea fleet, while Charles encamped at Budiszcze, between the Prol and the Worskla, two tributaries of the Don.

By this time the situation of the Swedes was not merely serious but alarming. The army had dwindled down from 41,000 to 20,000, of whom about 18,000 were able-bodied, the loss of superior officers being particularly ominous. To take only one instance, the six adjutant-generals, whom Charles had appointed on his departure from Saxony, had all perished. Supplies were running so short that it was as much as the men could do to keep body and soul together. Saltpetre had to be used now instead of salt, and there was not sufficient wine left to give the sacrament to the dying soldiers. All communication with Central Europe had been cut off by the Russians. The nearest Swedish army, Krassau's (when Charles quitted Saxony, he left Major-General Ernest Detlev Krassau with all the Swedish troops remaining in Poland. Krassau had orders to join the King in the Ukraine if possible, but was obliged to give up the idea as totally impracticable) was nine hundred miles away. Once more his officers tried to persuade Charles to return to Poland, so as to cooperate with Stanislaus and Krassau, but the King would not hear of such a thing because "a march back to the Dnieper would look like a flight and make the enemy all the bolder." He resolved instead to march still farther north, lay siege to the fortress of Pultawa, and there await the reinforcements he had ordered from Poland and Sweden, and solicited from Turkey and the Tartar Khan. What his ulterior plans were, it is impossible to say. Some think he had none at all, others suppose that, after giving his soldiers a long rest, he intended to make a second attempt upon Moscow. It was while on his way to Pultawa that Charles concluded an alliance with the Zaporogean Cossacks, who, as their name implies (Za—behind, porogo—a rapid or waterfall), dwelt behind the rapids of the Dnieper, southwards of the Ukrainian Cossacks, and had been persuaded by Mazepa to throw off the

Russian yoke. They now occupied most of the places to the south of Pultawa, while Charles took up a position to the north of that fortress. To attack it the Swedes were much too weak. It was not so much that his army had notably diminished (his Polish exploits had been performed with half as many men) as that he had next to no artillery left, and his powder was not only running short, but had so deteriorated with repeated wetting as to be almost useless. It is said that when a shot was fired off it sounded no louder than the clapping together of a pair of gloves, while the bullets fell down in the sand scarcely thirty paces from the mouth of the gun that fired them. There was such a dearth of bullets too, that the Swedes were glad to collect, and make use of, the spent balls of the enemy. And on the other side of the river Worskla, on which Pultawa is situated, lay the Tsar with an army four times as numerous as Charles', so that he was always able to throw provisions and reinforcements into the town. In May, 1709, the siege began.

CHAPTER 78

CHARLES WOUNDED

Charles did all in his power to encourage his men. He took up his quarters so close to the fortress that the walls of his house were literally riddled with bullets. When his engineer officers were shot down one after the other, he himself gave the sappers and miners the necessary instructions. Day by day the situation of the Swedes grew more distressing. The summer heat was oppressive, and caused most of the wounded to die of gangrene. The narrow district occupied by the Swedes was soon drained dry of food. At last the soldiers had nothing to eat but horseflesh and black bread. And now a fresh misfortune befell the besieging host, a misfortune but for which the culminating catastrophe might never have happened. Hitherto, although Charles had exposed himself to danger with such utter recklessness that many believed he was courting death, he had escaped unhurt, but on the 17th June, his birthday, he received a wound which placed him hors de combat. He was riding with Levenhaupt backwards and forwards along the banks of the Worskla, at break of day, within range of the fortress, when a bullet pierced his heel, passing through his foot, and finally lodging inside it, close to the great toe. The wound must have been a painful one, yet Charles did not so much as flinch, but continued riding about as if nothing had happened, though the blood dripped so fast from his boot that his attendants fancied at first that it was his horse that had been struck till the ghastly pallor of the King revealed the truth. Even then he would not return to his quarters till he had given some directions which took him over to the opposite end of the camp; when he did at last get back his foot was so swollen that the boot had to be cut off. On the foot being examined, it was found that several of the smaller bones had been crushed, and the surgeon hesitated to make the deep and painful incisions necessary for removing the splinters. "Come, come," cried Charles impatiently, "slash away, slash away!—it won't damage me!" and, firmly grasping his leg, he watched the operation through, without giving the slightest sign that he felt any pain. Nay, more, when, subsequently the lips of the wound swelled up, and the surgeons shrunk from cutting away the inflamed and exquisitely sensitive parts, advising instead the application of blue-stone, Charles asked for a pair of scissors, and cooly removed the affected parts himself. At first it was feared that gangrene would set in, and the King might lose his leg, especially as he obstinately refused for a long time to take drugs, but fortunately he was prevailed upon at last to swallow a sudorific, and the leg was saved. For all fighting purposes, however, Charles was not completely useless.

CHAPTER 79

PETER OUTNUMBERS MAZEPA

And it was just at this very time that his guidance was most wanted. Hitherto Peter, though he could oppose 80,000 to Charles' 18,000, had been careful to avoid every manoeuvre which might lead to a general engagement; but on hearing that Charles was "hors de combat", he immediately changed his tactics, and threw the greater part of his forces across the Worskla (June 19th - 23rd), though even now he was so diffident of himself and his troops in the presence of his great adversary, that he took the precaution to strongly entrench his camp. On the 24th June, he moved into a still stronger intrenched camp, closer to Pultawa, and on the 26th and 27th constructed a line of small field batteries, extending between the Swedish camp and his own. He evidently regarded mere numbers as an insufficient safeguard against the ragged veterans who had defeated him at Holowczyn and Krasnokutsk. Meanwhile Marshal Rehnskjold, who had taken over the supreme command of the Swedish army, held a council of war at which it was resolved at attack the Russians in their batteries and intrenched camp. Levenhaupt proposed that the useless siege of Pultawa should be raised, so that every available soldier might be sent to the front, but this Charles would not hear of, so observing the fortress. Add to this that 2,400 more had to be told off to guard the baggage, while 1,200 more were posted on the southern bank of the Worskla to prevent those of the Russians who had not yet crossed, from taking the Swedes in flank, and it will be seen that, not including the Zaporogean guerillas, who numbered about 6,000, Rehnskjold had barely 13,000 men at his disposal, and with these 13,000 he proposed to attack 80,000 men in a strongly intrenched camp! The council of war was held on the 26th June, and on the following day, Sunday, after evening prayers, all the generals were summoned to the King's bedside, and here the plan for the morrow's attack was definitely arranged. Then Charles had his wounded foot freshly bandaged, and drawing his spurred boot on the other, and taking his sword in his hand, he had himself borne in a litter through the ranks to the front, and finally took up his position amidst the guards, surrounded by Rehnskjold, Piper, Levenhaupt, and the other generals, who, wrapped in their mantles, lay or sat near the King's litter. Immediately after midnight Rehnskjold gave the order to break up, and advance nearer to the enemy's lines, and at dawn of day the Swedes saw the Russian bastions straight in front of them. The Swedish cavalry on the left wing was commanded by General Creutz, and here the King and Rehnskjold were posted; the centre, consisting of the infantry, was led by Levenhaupt, the cavalry on the right wing by Schlippenbach, while Axel Sparre and Carl Gustaf Roos were sent on in front to clear the way by capturing the enemy's line of field batteries. The Swedes, who had few cannons and wretched powder, reckoned chiefly on their swords; and at first things went well enough. Sparre captured the field batteries on the left by a gallant dash, and put the garrisons to the sword, and had Roos only been properly supported till he had captured the batteries on the right, the guns of all the Russian batteries could have been turned against the Russian intrenched camp, and, under cover of the fire, the whole Swedish army might have made a combined attack in perfect order. Unfortunately Piper, who had followed the King, advised "striking while the iron was hot, " by making Creutz follow up the advantage gained by Sparre, and the consequence was that the whole of the cavalry on the left wing advanced and scattered the Russian cavalry which stood behind the captured batteries, but at the same time left General Roos, whose duty it was to capture the batteries on the right, entirely unsupported. The Tsar perceived the blunder, and at once sent Menshikov with 10,000 Russians to cut off Roos who had already been thrice repulsed from the batteries in front of him, and was now completely surrounded and ultimately compelled to surrender after making an heoric resistance. Nevertheless the issue of the battle was still doubtful, for Levenhaupt with his infantry, although altogether without artillery, had captured two of the batteries in his way, and was preparing to storm the southern side of the enemy's intrenched camp, where it was weakest, at the point of the bayonet, when he received an order to halt. To this day it is not known who gave this order, but circumstances seem to point to the King as responsible for it, for when Rehnskjold, astonished and indignant that Levenhaupt should have stopped short at the very moment when victory seemed within his grasp, came rushing up and accused him of not acting as "a loyal servant of the King", Levenhaupt replied that he was only obeying orders, and at that moment Charles himself was borne to the spot in his litter. Then Rehnskjold, turning towards the King, exclaimed: "Is it your Majesty who ordered Levenhaupt to halt in front of the foe?" Charles colored up and answered, "No!" but in such a way as to make most of those present believe that he really had given the order. So at any rate Rehnskjold took it, and he made no secret of his indignation. "Yes, sir," cried he, "that's what you are always doing! I am never allowed to do what I would. For God's sake, sir, leave me to manage." Charles took the rebuke in perfect silence, and the whole Swedish army was re-formed in front of the hostile camp, which it was now to storm.

CHAPTER 80

MAZEPA'S MOMENT LOST FOREVER

But the favorable moment had gone. Peter, after the first successes of Creutz and Sparre, had been on the point of flying, but on perceiving the ridiculous numerical inferiority of the foe, his courage revived and he brought up every available man and gun to the front for final struggle. The Russian infantry numbered 40,000 men supported by 100 cannon, the Swedes had only 4,000 infantry, exhausted by hunger and fatigue, with bad powder, no artillery, nay, not even cavalry to support them, for, to Levenhaupt's amazement, Rehnskjold now posted his cavalry behind the infantry. Throughout the earlier part of the struggle Charles, sword in hand, had been carried through the lines, and done his utmost to encourage his men, utterly regardless of the rain of bullets that fell thickly around him. During the interval between the two engagements Charles rested a little, drank a glass of water, and had his foot rebandaged, after which he was again carried to the front. And now the signal to attack was given, and the heroic 4,000 rushed into certain death. The Russian fire was so terrible that before the Swedes could reach the intrenched camp, half their number already lay bleeding on the ground. With despair in their hearts, the remainder of the gallant little band rushed forward, and literally disappeared among the myriads of Russians who engulfed and overwhelmed them. Yet they sold their lives dearly, the guard in particular fighting with its usual doggedness, though it lost all it's officers in a few moments. Charles, to encourage his "blue boys", had had himself carried into fire, but the litter on which he lay was now smashed by a cannon-ball, he fell heavily to the ground, and twenty-one out of his twenty-four bearers were shot dead by his side. "My lads," cried Rehnskjold, who perceived that all was now lost, "save the King!" then he himself plunged into the thickest of the fight, and was shortly afterwards made a prisoner. Charles himself meanwhile was in the most imminent danger; indeed he owed his life entirely to the devotion of a Major Wolffelt, who lifted him on to his own horse, and was immediately afterwards cut to pieces by the

Cossacks. On this horse the King continued to ride about, with his wounded foot, which bled profusely, resting on the animal's neck. Presently he fell in with Levenhaupt. "What are we to do now!" enquired the King. "There is nothing for it but to try and collect the remains of our people in camp," replied the general. This they accordingly did, and the same evening what remained of the Swedish army quitted the field, the cavalry, which had suffered comparatively little, covering the retreat.

CHAPTER 81

PETER'S VICTORY OVER MAZEPA

The Russians are said to have lost 1,300 men at Pultawa, the Swedes 3,000 killed and 2,000 prisoners, among whom were one field-marshal, four major-generals, and five colonels. Count Piper, who had followed the King all day, and was separated from him in the final "melee", made his way up the the gates of Pultawa, and there voluntarily surrendered. Peter had fully expected to capture the Swedish King also. "Where is my brother Charles?" he asked repeatedly. He received the Swedish officers with respect and courtesy, but he asked Marshal Rehnskjold how he had dared to invade a great Empire like the Russian with a mere handful of men. Rehnskjold replied that the King had commanded it, and it was his first duty as a loyal subject to obey his Sovereign. "You are an honest fellow," replied the Tsar, "and for your loyalty I return you your sword."

Meanwhile, with banners flying and music playing, the Swedes had quitted Pultawa, and two days later reached Perewoloczna, an insignificant place on the Dnieper, situated on a narrow neck of land enclosed on three sides by that river and it's confluents. Here Charles, who was utterly exhausted by pain and fatigue, was persuaded, though only by the most urgent entreaties (Levenhaupt and Gyllenkrook went down on their knees before him, and besought him with tears in their eyes, to escape while there was yet time. Charles took with him his silver plate, and most of the treasure he had collected in Saxony), to cross the Dnieper some 1,500 cavalry, including Byllenkrook, Mazepa, and Secretary Mullern, and take refuge in Turkish territory, leaving Levenhaupt in command of the thoroughly cowed and demoralised mob that only twelve months before had been the finest army in Europe. Two days later Levenhaupt surrendered with the whole of his army (nearly 14,000 men) to the Russian general, Menshikov, who had in the meanwhile reached Perewoloczna, and effectively closed every loophole of retreat. Under the circumstances it was the best, or rather the only thing the unfortunate general could do, but Charles XII never forgave him for it. Thus Peter had triumphed at last. "The foundations of St. Petersburg are now firm and immovable!" he exclaimed when the struggle was over.

CHAPTER 82

MAZEPA & CHARLES' CROSS INTO TURKEY

After leaving the remains of his army at Perewoloczna, Charles crossed the Turkish border, hastening through the steppes towards the fortress of Oczakow on the Euxine. The little army suffered much from the intense heat and still more from hunger. The Zaporogeans lived on the flesh of the horses which they stole at night from their Swedish comrades, while the Swedes starved on black bread and wild cherries, and the King and his officers had nothing better than a little gurel and an occasional partridge, half-raosted on fires of dried horse-dung and grass. At Oczakow the pasha detained them on the opposite bank of the Bug, while he haggled over the price of the boats which were to carry them across, insisting on the extortionate price of 16 ducats a head, till the King, growing impatient, commanded his men to seize the boats by force. The delay caused thereby cost Charles 800 men, for it enabled the Russians to overtake the Swedish rear-guard, and cut them off to a man: sick, famished, and utterly exhausted, the remaining 500 made the best of their way to Bender on the Dniester, the most important Turkish fortress in those parts.

At Bender the Swedes rested at last from their long and painful journey, and enjoyed a comfort and luxury that they had not known for many years. Charles himself was received with every demonstration of respect and honor. The presence of Turkish soil of the most formidable antagonist of Turkey's mortal foe, Russia, was not displeasing to the Porte, and secret orders to treat the royal guest right royally seem to have been sent to the Seraskier of Bender, Jussuf Pasha, and the Tartar Khan, Devlet Gerai, who was also staying there at the time. And the wishes of the Khan and the Seraskier coincided with the commands of the Padishah. Both of them hated the Tsar, and both had a profound admiration for the King of Sweden. Splendid indeed was the hospitality which Charles now enjoyed. Sumptuous pavilions were provided for the Swedes on their arrival, the King and his soldiers were escorted to the town with great pomp and ceremony, and at the gate Jussuf presented to Charles the keys of the fortress, on his knees. During the summer the Swedes dwelt in tents near the Dniester, but on the approach of winter the Turks built huts and houses for them, while Charles ultimately erected for himself a large stone mansion, the walls of which were made several feet thick, so that it might serve as a fortress in case of need. Here he lived, with a court, a chancellery, a Janissary guard of honor, and all the appurtenances of royalty. Everything was conducted with military order and precision, even to divine service, which, held every morning and evening and thrice on Sundays, was duly announced from the royal balcony by a flourish of trumpets. Charles spent his time in reviewing and excercising his little army, transacting current business, playing chess, reading or listening to French tragedies (especially those of Corneille) and medieval romances of chivalry, and taking long and violent rides in the neighborhood, generally exhausting a couple of horses a day. At night he very often had fits of sleeplessness, and would then pay visits upon his officers and secretaries, and sit talking by their bedsides for hours. He gave them of his money without stint, but would never come to their banquets, contenting himself with looking through the windows at them when the mirth was growing fast and furious. At other times he would explore their rooms during their absence, ransack their drawers, and throw behind the fire all lace collars, embroidered vests and other frippery which did not correspond with his idea of soldierly simplicity in dress. On red-heeled shoes and slippers and fancy leather boots in particular he waged a relentless war. And here it should be remarked that the men Charles had about him at Bender were for the most part of subaltern rank or servile character, honest, devoted, laborious, and loyal no doubt, but obsequious, reckless or unprincipled, obeying implicitly orders they frequently knew to be mischievous, and never venturing to injure their own prospects by giving unpalatable advice.

CHAPTER 83

MAZEPA'S DEATH

The death of Mazepa (March 18, 1710), who was buried in the monastery of St. George at Galatz, the only person of any real eminence, both as to dignity and character. His tomb was rifled by the Tartars a few months later, and his bones scattered on the banks of the Danube.

Charles XII and the Collapse of the Swedish Empire (1682-1719) by R. Nisbet Bain; author of Gustavus of Sweden, written in 1895.

CHAPTER 84

INTRODUCTION

TO MAZEPA

Poem written in 1818 by
Lord Byron

Mazepa was written at Venice and Ravenna in the autumn of 1818. The story is a well-known one; of Mazepa, who, being bound naked on the back of a wild horse, on account of an intrigue with the lady of a certain great noble of his country, was carried by his steed into the heart of the Ukraine, and being picked up by some Cossacks, in a state apparently of utter hopelessness and exhaustion, recovered, and lived to be long after the prince and leader of the nation among whom he had arrived in this extraordinary manner.

Lord Byron has represented the strange and wild incidents of this adventure, as being related in half serious, half sportive way, by Mazepa himself, to no less a person than Charles the Twelfth of Sweden, in some of those last campaigns, the Cossack Hetman took a distinguished part. He tells it during the desolate bivouack of Charles and the few friends who fled with him towards Turkey, after the bloody overthrow of Pultava*. There is not a little of beauty and gracefulness in this way of setting the picture; —the age of Mazepa—the calm, practiced indifference with which he now submits to the worst of fortune's deeds—the heroic, unthinking coldness of the royal madman to whom he speaks—the dreary and perilous accompaniments of the scene around the speaker and the audience,—all contribute to throw a very striking charm both of preparation and of contrast over the wild story of the Hetman. Nothing can be more beautiful, in like manner, than the account of the love—the guilty love—the fruits of which had been so miraculous.

*Putlava is spelled this way in Western Europe.
*Putlawa is spelled this way in Eastern Europe.

MAZEPA

I.

'Twas after dread Pultow's day,
  When Fortune left the royal Swede—
Around a slaughtered army lay,
  No more to combat and to bleed.
The power and glory of the war,
  Faithless as their vain votaries, men,
Had passed to the triumphant Czar,
  And Moscow's walls were safe again—
Until a day more dark and drear,
And a more memorable year,
Should give to slaughter and to shame
A mightier host and haughtier name;
A greater wreck, a deeper fall
A shock to one—a thunderbolt to all.

II.

Such was the hazard of the die;
The wounded Charles was taught to fly
By day and night through field and flood,
Strained with his own subjects' blood;
For thousands fell that flight to aid:
And not a voice was heard to up braid
Ambition in his humbled hour,
When Truth had nought to dread from Power.
His horse was slain, and Gieta gave
His own—and died the Russians' slave.
This, too, sinks after many aleague
Of well-sustained, but vain fatigue;
And in the depth of forests darkling,
The watch-fires in the distance sparkling—
The beacons of surrounding foes—
A king must lay his limbs at length.
Are these the laurels and repose
For which the nations strain their strength?

They laid him by a savage tree,
In outworn Nature's agony;
His wounds were stiff, his limbs were stark;
The heavy hour was chill and dark;
The fever in his blood forbade
A transient slumber's fitful aid:
And thus it was; but yet through all,
Kinglike the monarch bore his fall,
And made, in this extreme of ill,
His pangs the vassals of his will:
All silent and subdued were they,
As once the nations round him lay.

III.

A band of chiefs !—alas ! how few,
  Since but the fleeting of a day
Had thinned it; but this wreck was   true
  And chivalrous: upon the clay
Each sate him down, all sad and mute,
Beside his monarch and his steed;
For danger levels man and brute,
And all are fellows in their need.
Among the rest, Mazepa made
His pillow in an old oak's shade—
Himself as rough, and scarce less old,
The Ukraine's Hetman, calm and bold;
But first, outspent with this long course,
The Cossack prince rubbed down his horse,
And made for him a leafy bed,
And smoothed his fetlocks and his mane,
And slacked his girth, and stripped his rein,
And joyed to see how well he fed;
For until now he had the dread
His wearied courser might refuse
To browse beneath the midnight dews:
But he was hardy as his lord,
And little cared for bed and board;
But spirited and docile too,

Whate'er was to be done, would do.
Shaggy and swift, and strong of limb,
All Tartar-like he carried him;
Obeyed his voice, and came to call,
And knew him in the midst of all:
Though thousands were around, —and Night,
Without a star, pursued her flight,—
That steed from sunset until dawn
His chief would follow like a fawn.
This down, Mazepa spread his cloak,
And laid his lance beneath his oak,
Felt if his arms in order good
The long day's march had well with stood—
If still the powder filled the pan,
And flints unloosened kept their lock—
His sabre's hilt and scabbard felt,
And whether they had chafed his belt;
And next the venerable man,
From out his havresack and can,
Prepared and spread his slender stock;
And to the Monarch and his men
The whole or portion offered then
With far less of inquietude
Than courtiers at a banquet would.
And Charles of this his slender share
With smiles partook a moment there,
To force of cheer a greater show,
And seem above both wounds and woe;—
  and then he said—"Of all our band,
Though firm of heart and strong of hand,
In skirmish, march, or forage, none
Can less have said or more have done
Than thee, Mazepa! On the earth
So fit a pair had never birth,
Since Alexander's days till now,
As they Bucephalus and thou:
All Scythia's fame to thine should yield
For pricking on o'er flood and field."

Mazepa answered—"I'll betide
The school wherin I learned to ride!"
Quoth Charles—"Old Hetman, where fore so,
Since thou hast learned the art so well?"
Mazepa said—"'Twere long to tell;
And we have many a league to go,
With every now and then a blow,
And ten to one at least the foe,
Before our steeds may graze at ease,
Beyond the swift Borysthenes:
And, Sire, your limbs have need of rest,
And I will be the sentinel
Of this your troop."—"But I request,"
Said Sweden's monarch, "thou wilt tell
This tale of thine, and I may reap,
Perchance, from this the boon of sleep;
For at this moment from my eyes
The hope of present slumber flies."

"Well, Sire, with such a hope, I'll track
My seventy years of memory back:
I think 'twas in my twentieth spring,—
Aye 'twas,—when Casimir was king—
John Casimir,—I was his page
Six summers, in my earlier age:
A learned monarch, faith! was he,
And most unlike your Majesty;
He made no wars, and did not gain
New realms to lose them back again;
And (save debates in Warsaw's diet)
He reigned in most unseemly quiet;
Not that he had no cares to vex;
He loved the Muses and the Sex;
And sometimes these so froward are,
They made him wish himself at war;
But soon his wrath being o'er, he took
Another mistress-or new book:
And then he gave prodigious fetes—

All Warsaw gathered round his gates
To gaze upon his splendid court,
And dames, and chiefs, of princely port.
He was the Polish Solomon,
So sung his poets, all but one,
Who, being unpensioned, made a satire,
And boasted that he could not flatter.
It was a court of jousts and mimes,
Where every courtier tried at rhymes;
Even I for once produced some verses,
And signed my odes 'Despairing Thyrsis.'
There was a certain Palatine,
A Count of far and high descent,
Rich as a salt or silver mine;
And he was proud, ye may divine,
As if from Heaven he had been sent;
He had such wealth in blood and ore
As few could match beneath the throne;
And he would gaze upon his store,
And o'er his pedigree would pore,
Until by some confusion led,
Which almost looked like want of head,
He thought their merits were his own.
His wife was not of this opinion;
His junior she by thirty years,
Grew daily tired of his dominion;
And, after wishes, hopes, and fears,
To Virtue a few farewell tears,
A restless dream or two—some glances
At Warsaw's youth—some songs, and dances,
Awaited but the usual chances,
Those happy accidents which render
The coldest dames so very tender,
To deck her Count with titles given,
'Tis said, as passports into Heaven;
But, strange to say, they rarely boast
Of these, who have deserved them most.

V.

I was a goodly stripling then;
At seventy years I so may say,
That there were few, or boys or men,
Who, in my dawning time of day,
Of vassal or of knight's degree,
Could vie in vanities with me;
For I had strength—youth—gaiety,
A port, not like to this ye see,
But smooth, as all is rugged now;
For Time, and Care, and War, have ploughed
My very soul from out my brow;
And thus I should be disavowed
By all my kind and kin, could they
Compare my day and yesterday;
This change was wrought, too, long   ere age
Had ta'en my features for his page:
With years, ye know, have not declined
My strength—my courage—or my mind,
Or at this hour I should not be
telling old tales beneath a tree,
With starless skies my canopy.
But let me on: Theresa's form—
Methinks it glides before me now,
Between me and yon chestnut's bough,
The memory is so quick and warm;
And yet I find no words to tell
The shape of her I loved so well:
She had the Asiatic eye,
Such as our Turkish neighborhood
Hath mingled with our Polish blood,
Dark as above us in the sky;
But through it stole a tender light,
Like the first moonrise of midnight;
Large, dark, and swimming in the stream,
Which seemed to melt to its own beam;
All love, half languor, and half fire,

Like saints that at the stake expire,
And lift their raptured looks on high,
As though it were a joy to die.
A brow like a midsummer lake,
Transparent with the sun therein,
When waves no murmur dare to make,
And heaven beholds her face within.
A cheek and lip—but why proceed?
I loved her then, I love her still;
And such as I am, love indeed
In fierce extreme's—in good and ill.
But still we love even in our rage,
And haunted to our very age
With the vain shadow of the past,—
As is Mazepa to the last.

VI.

"We met—we gazed—I saw, and sighed;
She did not speak, and yet replied;
There are ten thousand tones and signs
We hear and see, but none defines—
Involuntary sparks of thought,
Which strike from out the heart o'erwrought,
And form a strange intelligence,
Alike mysterious and intense,
Which link the burning chain that binds,
Without their will, young hearts and minds;
Conveying, as the electric wire,
We know not how, the absorbing fire.
I saw, and sighed—in silence wept,
And still reluctant distance kept,
Until I was made known to her,
And we might then and there confer
Without suspicion—then, even then,
I longed, and was resolved to speak;
But on my lips they died again,
The accents tremulous and weak,
Until on hour.—There is a game,

A frivolous and foolish play.
Wherewith we while away the day;
It is—I have forgot the name—
And we to this, it seems, were set,
By some strange chance, which I forget:
I recked not if I won or lost,
It was enough for me to be
No near to hear, and oh! to see
The being whom I loved the most.
I watched her as a sentinel,
(May ours this dark night watch as well!)
Until I saw, and thus it was,
That she was pensive, nor perceived
Her occupation, nor was grieved
Nor glad to lose or gain; but still
Played on for hours, as if her will
Yet bound her to the place, though not
That hers might be he winning lot.
Then through my brain the thought did pass,
Even as a flash of lightning there,
That there was something in her air
Which would not doom me to despair;
And on the thought my words broke forth,
All incoherent as they were;
Their eloquence was little worth,
But yet she listened—'tis enough—
Who listens once will listen twice;
Her heart, be sure, is not of ice—
And one refusal no rebuff.

VII.

"I loved, and was beloved again—
They tell me, Sire, you never knew
Those gentle frailties; if 'tis true,
I shorten all my joy or pain;
To you 'twould seem absurd as vain;
But all men are not born to reign,
Or o'er their passions, or as you

Thus o'er themselves and nations too.
I am—or rather was—a Prince,
A chief of thousands, and could lead
Them on where each would foremost bleed;
But could not o'er myself evince
The like control—But to resume:
I loved, and was beloved again;
In sooth, it is a happy doom,
But yet where happiest ends in pain.—
We met in secret, and the hour
Which led me to that lady's bower
Was fiery Expectation's dower.
My days and nights were nothing—all
Except that hour which doth recall,
In the long lapse from youth to age,
No other like itself: I'd give
The Ukraine back again to live
It o'er once more, and be a page,
The happy page, who was the lord
Of one soft heart, and his own sword,
And had no other gem nor wealth,
Save Nature's give of Youth and Health.
We met in secret—doubly sweet,
Some say, they find it so to meet;
I know not that—I would have given
My life but to have called her mine
In the full view of Earth and Heaven;
For I did oft and long repine
That we could only meet by stealth.

VIII.

"For lovers there are many eyes,
And such there were on us; the Devil
On such occasions should be civil—
The Devil!—I'm loth to do him wrong,
It might be some untoward saint,
Who would not be at rest too long,
But to his pious bile gave vent—

But one fair night, some lurking spies
Surprised and seized us both.
The Count was something more than wroth—
I was unarmed; but if in steel,
All cap-a-pie from head to heel,
What 'gainst their numbers could I do?
'Twas near his castle, far away
From city or from succour near,
And almost on the break of day;
I did not think to see another,
My moments seemed reduced to few;
And with one prayer to Mary Mother,
And, it may be, a saint or two,
As I resigned me to my fate,
They led me to the castle gate:
Theresa's doom I never knew,
Our lot was henceforth separate.
An angry man, ye may opine,
Was he, the proud Count Palatine;
And he had reason good to be,
But he was most enraged lest such
An accident should chance to touch
Upon his future pedigree;
Norless amazed, that such a blot
His noble 'scutcheon should have got,
While he was highest of his line;
Because unto himself he seemed
The first of men, nor less he deemed
In others' eyes, and most in mine.
'Sdeath! with a page-perchance a king
Had reconciled him to the thing;
But with a stripling of a page—
I felt—but cannot paint his rage.

IX.

"'Bring forth the horse!'—the horse was brought!
In truth, he was a noble steed,
A Tartar of the Ukraine breed,

Who looked as though the speed of thought
Were in his limbs; but he was wild,
Wild as the wild deer, and untaught,
With spur and bridle undefiled—
'Twas but day he had been caught;
And snorting, with erected mane,
And struggling fiercely, but in vain,
In the full foam of wrath and dread
To me the desert-born was led:
They bound me on, that menial throng,
Upon his back with many a thong;
They losed him with a sudden lash—
Away! away!—and on we dash!—
Torrents less rapid and less rash.

X.

"Away!—away !—My breath was gone,
I saw not where he hurried on:
'Twas scarcely yet the break of day,
And on he foamed—away !—away !
The last of human sounds which rose,
As I was darted from my foes,
Was the wild shout of savage laughter,
Which on the wind came roaring after
A moment from that rabble route:
With sudden wrath I wrenched my head,
And snapped the cord, which to the mane
Had bound my neck in lieu of rein,
And, writhing half my form about,
Howled back my curse; but 'midst the tread,
The thunder of my courser's speed,
Perchance they did not hear nor heed:
It vexes me—for I would fain
Have paid their insult back again.
I paid it well in after days:
There is not of that castle gate,
Its drawbridge and portcullis' weight,
Stone—bar—moat—bridge—or barrier left;

Nor of its fields a blade of grass,
Save what grows on a ridge of wall,
Where stood the hearth-stone of the hall;
And many a time ye there might pass,
Nor dream that e'er the fortress was.
I saw its turrets in a blaze,
Their crackling battlements all cleft,
And the hot lead pour down like rain
From off the scorched and blackening roof
Whose thickness was not vengeance-proof.
They little thought that day of pain,
When launched, as on the lightning's flash,
They bade me to destruction dash,
That one day I should come again,
With twice five thousand horse, to thank
The Count for his uncourteous ride.
They played me then a bitter prank,
When, with the wild horse for my guide,
They bound me to his foaming flank;
At length I played them one as frank—
For Time at last sets all things even—
And if we do but watch the hour,
There never yet was human power
Which could evade, if unforgiven,
The patient search and vigil long
Of him who treasures up a wrong.

XI.

"Away!—away!—my steed and I,
Upon the pinions of the wind!
All human dwellings left behind,
We sped like meteors through the sky,
When with its crackling sound the night
Is chequered with the Northern light.
Town—village—none were on our track,
But a wild plain of far extent,
And bounded by a forest black;
And, save the scarce seen battlement

On distant heights of some strong hold,
Against the Tartars built of old,
No trace of man. The year before
A Turkish army had marched o'er;
And where the Spahi's hoof hath trod,
The verdure flies the bloody sod:
The sky was dull, and dim, and gray,
And a low breeze crept moaning by—
I could have answered with a sigh—
But fast we fled,—away!—away!—
And I could neither sigh nor pray;
And my cold sweat-drops fell like
rain upon the courser's bristling mane;
But, snorting still with rage and fear,
He flew upon his far career;
At times I almost thought, indeed,
He must have slackened in his speed;
But no—my bound and slender frame
Was nothing to his angry might,
And merely like a spur became:
Each motion which I made to free
My swoln limbs from their agony
Increased his fury and affright:
I tried my voice,—'twas faint and low—
But yet he swerved as from a blow;
And, starting to each accent, sprang
As from a sudden trumpet's clang:
Meantime my cords were wet with gore,
Which, oozing through my limbs, ran o'er;
And in my tongue the thirst became
A something fierier far than flame.

XII.

"We neared the wild wood—'twas so wide,
I saw no bounds on either side:
'twas studded with old sturdy trees,
That bent not to the roughest breeze
Which howls down from Siberia's waste,

And strips the forest in it's haste,—
But these were few and far between,
Set thick with shrubs more young and green,
Luxuriant with their annual leaves,
Ere strown by those autumnal eves
That nip the forest's foliage dead,
Discolored with a lifeless red,
Which stands thereon like stiffened gore
Upon the slain when battle's o'er;
And some long winter's night hath shed
Its frost o'er every tombless head—
So cold and stark—the raven's beak
May peck unpierced each frozen cheek:
'Twas a wild waste of underwood,
And here and there a chestnut stood,
The strong oak, and the hardy pine;
But far apart—and well it were,
Or else a different lot were mine—
The boughs gave way, and did not tear
My limbs; and I found strength to bear
My wounds, already scarred with cold;
My bonds forbade to loose my hold.
We rustled through the leaves like wind,—
Left shrubs, and trees, and wolves behind;
By night I heard them on the track,
Their troop came hard upon our back,
With their long gallop, which can tire
The hound's deep hate, and hunter's fire:
Where'er we flew they followed on,
Nor left us with the morning sun;
Behind I saw them, scarce a rood,
At day-break winding through the wood,
And through the night had heard their feet
Their stealing, rustling step repeat.
Oh! how I wished for spear or sword,
At least to die amidst the horde,
And perish—it if must be so—
At bay, destroying many a foe!

When first my courser's race begun,
I wished the goal already won;
But now I doubted strength and speed:
Vain doubt! his swift and savage breed
Had nerved him like the mountain-roe—
Nor faster falls the blinding snow
Which whelms the peasant near the door
Whose threshold he shall cross no more,
Bewildered with the dazzling blast,
Than through the forest-paths he passed—
Untired, untamed, and worse than wild—
All furious as a favoured child
Balked of it's wish; or—fiercer still—
A woman piqued—who has her will!

XIII.

"The wood was passed; 'twas more than noon,
But chill the air, although in June;
Or it might be my veins ran cold—
Prolonged endurance tames the bold;
And I was then not what I seem,
But headlong as a wintry stream,
And wore my feelings out before
I well could count their causes o'er:
And what with fury, fear, and wrath,
The tortures which beset my path—
Cold-hunger—sorrow—shame—distress—
Thus bound in Nature's nakedness;
Sprung from a race whose rising blood
When stirred beyond its calmer mood,
And trodden hard upon, is like
The rattle-snake's, in act to strike—
What marvel if this worn-out trunk
Beneath its woes a moment sunk?
The earth gave way, the skies rolled round,
I seemed to sink upon the ground;
But erred—for I was fastly bound.
My heart turned sick, my brain grew sore,

And throbbed awhile, then beat no more:
The skies spun like a mighty wheel;
I saw the trees like drunkards reel,
And a slight flash sprang o'er my eyes,
Which saw no farther. He who dies
Can die no more than then I died,
O'ertortured by that ghastly ride.
I felt the blackness come and go,

And strove to wake; but could not make
My senses climb up from below:
I felt as on a plank at sea,
When all the waves that dash o'er thee,
At the same time upheave and whelm,
And hurl thee towards a desert realm.
My undulating life was as
The fancied lights that flitting pass
Our shut eyes in deep midnight, when
Fever begins upon the brain;
But soon it passed, with little pain,
But a confusion worse than such:
I own that I should deem it much,
Dying, to feel the same again;
And yet I do suppose we must
Feel far more ere we turn to dust!
No matter! I have bared my brow
Full in Death's face—before—and now.

XIV.

"My thoughts came back. Where was I? Cold
And numb, and giddy: pulse by pulse
Life reassumed its lingering hold,
And throb by throb,—til grown a pang
Which for a moment would convulse,
My blood reflowed, though thick and chill;
My ear with uncouth noises rang,
My heart began once more to thrill;
My sight returned, though dim; alas!

And thickened, as it were, with glass.
Methought the dash of waves was nigh;
There was a gleam too of the sky,
Studded with stars;—it is no dream;
The wild horse swims the wilder stream!
The bright broad river's gushing tide
Sweeps, winding onward, far and wide,
And we are half-way, struggling o'er
To yon unknown and silent shore.
The waters broke my hollow trance,
And with a temporary strength
My stiffened limbs were rebaptized.
My courser's broad breast proudly braves,
And dashes off the ascending waves,
And onward we advance!
We reach the slippery shore at length,
A haven I but little prized,
For all behind was dark and drear,
And all before was night and fear.
How many hours of night or day
In those suspended pangs I lay,
I could not tell; I scarcely knew
If this were human breath I drew.

XV.

"With glossy skin, and dripping mane,
And reeling limbs, and reeking flank,
The wild steed's sinewy nerves still strain
Up the repelling bank.
We gain the top: a boundless plain
Spreads through the shadow of the night,
And onward, onward, onward—seems,
Like precipices in our dreams,
To stretch beyond the sight;
And here to there a speck of white,
Or scattered spot of dusky green,
In masses broke into the light,
As rose the moon upon my right:

But nought distinctly seen
In the dim waste would indicate
The omen of a cottage gate;
No twinkling taper from afar
Stood like a hospitable star;
Not even an ignis-fatuus rose
To make him merry with my woes:
That very cheat had cheered me then!
Although detected, welcome still,
Reminding me, through every ill,
Of the abodes of men.

XVI.

"Onward we went—but slack and slow;
His savage force at length o'erspent,
The drooping courser, faint and low,
All feebly foaming went:
A sickly infant had had power
To guide him forward in that hour!
But, useless all to me,
His new-born tameness nought availed—
My limbs were bound; my force had failed,
Perchance, had they been free.
With feeble effort still I tried
To rend the bonds so starkly tied,
But still it was in vain;
My limbs were only wrung the more,
And soon the idle strife gave o'er,
Which but prolonged their pain.
The dizzy race seemed almost done,
Although no goal was nearly won:
Some streaks announced the coming sun—
How slow, alas! he came!
Methought that mist of dawning gray
Would never dapple into day,
How heavily it rolled away!
Before the eastern flame
Rose crimson, and deposed the stars,

And called the radiance from their cars,
And filled the earth, from his deep throne,
With lonely lustre, all his own.

XVII.

"Uprose the sun; the mists were curled
Back from the solitary world
Which lay around—behind—before.
What booted it to traverse o'er
Plain—forest—river? Man nor brute,
Nor dint of hood, nor print of foot,
Lay in the wild luxuriant soil—
No sign of travel, none of toil—
The very air was mute:
And not an insect's shrill small horn,
Nor matin bird's new voice was borne
From herb nor thicket. Many a werst,
Panting as if his heart would burst,
The weary brute still staggered on;
And still we were—or seemed—alone;
At length, while reeling on our way,
Methought I heard a courser neigh,
From out yon tuft of blackening firs.
Is it the wind those branches stirs?
No, no! from out the forest prance
A trampling troop; I see them come!
In one vast squadron they advance!
I strove to cry—my lips were dumb!
The steeds rush on in plunging pride;
But where are they the reins to guide?
A thousand horse, and none to ride!
With flowing tail, and flying mane,
Wide nostrils never stretched by pain,
Mouths bloodless to the bit or rein,
And feet that iron never shod,
And flanks unscarred by spur or rod,
A thousand horse, the wild, the free,
Like waves that follow o'er the sea,

Came thickly thundering on,
As if our faint approach to meet!
The sight re-nerved my courser's feet,
A moment staggering, feebly fleet,
A moment, with a faint low neigh,
He answered, and then fell!
With gasps and glazing eyes he lay,
And reeking limbs immoveable,
His first and last career is done!
On came the troop—they saw him stoop,
They saw me strangely bound along
His back with many a bloody thong.
They stop—they start—they snuff the air,
Gallop a moment here and there,
Approach, retire, wheel round and round,
Then plunging back with sudden bound,
Headed by one black mighty steed,
Who seemed the Patriarch of his breed,
Without a single speck or hair
Of white upon his shaggy hide;
They snort—the foam—neigh—swerve aside,
And backward to the forest fly,
By instinct, from a human eye.
They left me there to my despair,
Linked to the dead and stiffening wretch,
Whose lifeless limbs beneath me stretch,
Relieved from that unwonted weight,
From whence I could not extricate
Nor him nor me—and there we lay,
The dying on the dead!
I little deemed another day
Would see my houseless, helpless head.

"And there from morn to twilight bound,
I felt the heavy hours toil round,
With just enough of life to see
My last of suns go down on me,
In hopeless certainty of mind,

That makes us feel at length resigned
To that which our foreboding years
Present the worst and last of fears:
Inevitable—even a boon,
Nor more unkind for coming soon,
Yet shunned and dreaded with such care,
As if it only were a snare
That Prudence might escape:
At times both wished for and implored,
At times sought with self-pointed sword,
Yet still a dark and hideous close
To even intolerable woes,
And welcome in no shape.
And, strange to say, the sons of pleasure,
They who have revelled beyond measure
In beauty, wassail, wine, and treasure,
Die calm, or calmer, oft than he
Whose heritage was Misery.
For he who hath in turn run through
All that was beautiful and new,
Hath nought to hope, and nought to leave;
And, save the future, (which is viewed
Not quite as men are base or good,
But as their nerves may be endued,)
With nought perhaps to grieve:
The wretch still hopes his woes must end,
And Death, whom he should deem his friend,
Appears, to his distempered eyes,
Arrived to rob him of his prize,
The tree of his new Paradise.
To-morrow would have given him all,
Repaid his pangs, repaired his fall;
To-morrow would have been the first
Of days no more deplored or curst,
But bright, and long, and beckoning years,
Seen dazzling through the mist of tears,
Guerdon of many a painful hour;
To-morrow would have given him power

To rule—to shine—to smile—to save—
And must it dawn upon his grave?

XVIII.

"The sun was sinking—still I lay
Chained to the chill and stiffening steed!
I thought to mingle there our clay;
And my dim eyes of death had need,
No hope arose of being freed.
I cast my last looks up the sky,
And there between me and the sun
I saw the expecting raven fly,
Who scarce would wait till both should die,
Ere his repast begun;
He flew, and perched, then flew once more,
And each time nearer than before;
I saw his wing through twilight flit,
And once so near me he alit
I could have smote, but lacked the strength;
But the slight motion of my hand,
And feeble scratching of the sand,
The exerted throat's faint struggling noise,
Which scarcely could be called a voice,
Together scared him off at length.
I know no more—my latest dream
Is something of a lovely star
Which fixed my dull eyes from afar,
And went and came with wandering beam,
And of the cold—dull—swimming—dense
Sensation of recurring sense,
And then subsiding back to death,
And then again a little breath,
A little thrill—a short suspense,
An icy sickness curdling o'er
My heart, and sparks that crossed my brain—
A gasp—a throb—a start of pain,
A sigh—and nothing more.

XIX.

"I woke—where was I?—Do I see
A human face look down on me?
And doth a roof above me close?
Do these limbs on a couch repose?
Is this a chamber where I lie?
And is it mortal yon bright eye,
That watches me with gentle glance?
I closed my own again once more,
As doubtful that my former trance
Could not as yet be o'er.
A slender girl, long-haired, and tall,
Sate watching by the cottage wall.
The sparkle of her eye I caught,
Even with my first return of thought;
For ever and anon she threw
A prying, pitying glance on me
With her black eyes so wild and free;
I gazed, and gazed, until I knew
No vision it could be,—
But that I lived, and was released
From adding to the vulture's feast:
And when the Cossack maid beheld
My heavy eyes at length unsealed,
She smiled—and I essayed to speak,
But failed—and she approached, and made
With lip and finger signs that said,
I must not strive as yet to break
The silence, till my strength should be
Enough to leave my accents free;
And then her hand on mine she laid,
And smoothed the pillow for my head,
And stole along on tiptoe tread,
And gently oped the door, and spake
In whispers—ne'er was voice so sweet!
Even music followed her light feet.
But those she called were not awake,

And she went forth; but, ere she passed,
Another look on me she cast,
Another sign she made, to say,
That I had nought to fear, that all
Were near, at my command or call,
And she could not delay
Her due return:—while she was gone,
Me thought I felt too much alone.

XX.

"She came with mother and with sire—
What need of more?—I will not tire
With long recital of the rest,
Since I became the Cossack's guest.
They found me senseless on the plain,
They bore me to the nearest hut,
They brought me into life again—
Me—one day o'er their realm to reign!
Thus the vain fool who strove to glut
His rage, refining on my pain,
Sent me forth to the wilderness,
Bound—naked—bleeding—and alone,
To pass the desert to a throne,—
What mortal his own doom may guess?
Let none despond, let none despair!
To-morrow the Borysthenes
May see our coursers graze at ease
Upon his Turkish bank,—and never
Had I such welcome for a river
As I shall yield when safely there.
Comrades, good night!"—The Hetman threw
His length beneath the oak-tree shade,
With leafy couch already made—
A bed nor comfortless nor new
To him, who took his rest whene'er
The hour arrived, no matter where:
His eyes the hastening slumbers steep.
And if ye marvel Charles forgot

To thank his tale, he wondered not,—
The King had been an hour asleep!

CHAPTER 85

DR. S. C. MAZEPA'S FORWARD
TO PUSHKIN'S MAZEPA

Lord Byron was a Westerner, an Englishman, who wrote of
Mazepa in 1818, and yet 11 years later, Pushkin comes along. In
the true sense a Black Russian; a man who spent many a day drinking black coffee and vodka in coffee houses. He was born in
Moscow in 1799. A real Russian writer. On his father's side he
was a descendant from an old aristocratic family of true Russians.

But his maternal great-grandfather was a real negro from
Abyssinia. Later in life Pushkin liked to allude to his African roots,
and even wrote a book about his proud Black ancestors.

His writings in praise of liberty and freedom from slavery,
whether it was serfdom or black slavery, to him it was all the same.
Slavery was slavery. His sharp epigrams against famous dignitaries
of the church and state, led to his exile in 1820 to a government post
in distant Bessarabia. In 1826, Pushkins banishment came to an
end. But he was still not allowed to travel abroad and he remained
politically suspect to his last days.

Pushkin knew the rage of love. His wife who was considered a beauty by Russians standards drove him to jealousy. He
began to doubt his wife's fidelity. He went so far to provoke one
of her most persistent admirers, Baron Heckeren-d Anthes to chal-
lenge him. In the duel, Pushkin was fatally wounded. But, before
he did die, he retold folk tales and retranslated them from several
languages. He put together a history of Mazepa to inspire popular
rebellion, and ventured into criticism and journalism. In Poltava,
about Mazepa, he broke new ground and was called a master by
Russian critics. He was referred to as the purest and noblest

expressions of Russia's literary genius.

At the time of this poem story, Russian literature was only beginning to emerge from the Russian court. This poem, Poltava, which is about Mazepa and his fight for Ukrainian Independence, which at the time of Pushkin was an affair of the Russian court; practically unknown to the rest of the world.

Most of us only remember WWII. But up until 1904 during the Russo-Japanese War, that Russia had a claim of being a country of military glory, and since the reigns of Peter the Great, Russia never lost a war. During the Crimean War, where all alone Russia was competing with the rest of Europe. All the greatest conquerors of Europe (Charles the Twelfth, Fredrich the Great, the French Revolutionary Armies, the troops of Napoleon the Great, WWI, Germany WWII the Nazi's, all went down to defeat when Confronted by the Russian armies. So I feel it should not be a surprise to discover that no poet has so vividly and gorgeously depicted the battlefield and war as Pushkin.

For a long time I considered Pushkin a kind of continuation of the genius of Pushkin in another person. This person being Mazepa. Their lifestyles in thinking. As if I can emphasize their sameness. Both Mazepa and Pushkin met their death in the same manner, in a duel. Mazepa's duel was with his desire for the independence of the Ukraine. For me to eulogize both Mazepa and Pushkin in military oligarchy. Both of them found themselves at last in disfavor in the Russian court proves my thinking on this matter during my entire lifetime of thinking. I find it easy to define Pushkin as he evinced himself in Poltava. He was fully justified in writing about Mazepa in Poltava.

Pushkin still remains one of our common humanity. It might surprise some readers of Mazepa, that judging from the complete victory of the communists in Russia from the October Revolution up until the fall of the Berlin Wall and the internal destruction of the Soviet Union; that Pushkin knew, as did Mazepa.

The Ukrainians no longer ponder over the theories of class-struggle and the five-year plans of industry, but directed their attention to the beliefs of the people and to the character and psychology of freedom. Freedom of the Ukraine arrived just in time as if per schedule and the origin of that freedom began with Mazepa.

CHAPTER 86

ALEKSANDR SERGEEVICH PUSHKIN
1799 - 1837
Russian Writer; Born in Moscow

Poem of Poltava

One of the purest and noblest expression of Russia's literary genius.

Pushkin knows Mazepa, though he really does not understand him. But Pushkin knew that Mazepa would never be understood by the average man.

Being a Mazepa, I can understand Mazepa's character. A man who rose from obscurity to the highest office in his country, gained for himself the woman he loved, for which there is nothing left in life except the woman a man loves and respects.

Yet, Mazepa threw everything away on a crazy gamble. The only comment the average man would make is that false pride comes before a fall, and when this happens, the mind and judgement become obscure. Because Independence for the Ukraine comes before your personal goals, and this is the great gamble Mazepa based his life upon. Yet, today almost 300 years later, the struggle for Ukrainian independence, survival and freedom are sparked from these original emotions that Mazepa had then.

POLTAVA

DEDICATION

To thee:
Wilt thou thine ear lend,
Listen to the songs of thy bard?
Will thy modest soul understand
The aspirations of my heart;
Or wilt thou, the poet's dedication,
As once his infatuation
Unrecognized, disdain,
And will it again
Unanswered remain?
At least these sounds hear,
Once to thee so dear,
And think:
That the last word of thee,
Of our last day of parting,
Is still my treasure and sanctity,
My only love for thee.

PART I.

Rich and powerful Kochubey,
His meads spread for away,
His countless herds of horses graze unguarded.
All around Poltava, his houses are engirth by many gardens.
Many riches doth he hold:
Furs, satins, gold,
On sight and under locks.
But proud is this lord,
Not of his long-maned horses, flocks,
Not of gold, tribute of Crimean horde,
But of a daughter, fair as day,
Is proud, old Kochubey.

'Tis true: In Poltava none so fair
Is found with Maria to compare.
Fresh as the spring flower,

Nurtured in the shadow of a bower,
Straight as a poplar of the Kiev Height.
Her movements are light
As those of a swan of the rivers bright,
As of a swift gazelle in her flight.
Like foam, her breasts are white.
Round her high forehead,
Black locks like clouds spread.
Like roses her lips are red.
Like the stars shine her eyes.
Not only beauty, gossip to her ascribes,—
Not only for her beauty is she famed:
"A sensible, modest maid," she's named.
And enviable grooms, does send
To her all parts of Russia's land.
But a bridal crown, like chains,
The timid maid disdians.
At last the Hetman, too, himself sends
His request through his friends.
He is old and bowed with years,
With worries of war and work and fears;
But passions still are burning in him:
Mazepa knows love again.
A youth's love is but a whim;
It doth not last with him;
It comes and disappears again.
Not so is the love an old man long   restrained
And hardened
By his years. Love's flame
In him but slowly, stubbornly, is fanned;
And if once the old man it does claim,
With him forever it does remain;
It comes to him to stay,
With death only will it pass away.

No gazelle behind the cliff doth hide,
While hearing of the earle's heavy   flight;
Trembling fearfully with expectation,

In the shadows strays the bride.
But her mother, full of indignation,
Comes to her, enfolds her in embrace.
"Impudent old man!" she says.
"How shameless thus for the Hetman to connive!
No, not as long as we are alive
Will his name with this crime be stained.
He should be ashamed! A father and a friend,
He ought to be to his own god-child so innocent.
Madman, with his lifetime reaching its end,
He aspires to be thy husband."

Maria trembled, deathlike paleness
Came over face.
Turning cold and lifeless,
She dropped on the staircase.

She did from her faint rise,
But again she closed her eyes.
Father, mother,
Then sought to console her,
Her confused worries to erase
In vain. Two days
She did not eat or drink.
Pale as a shadow, she strayed
Silent, crying, sighing.
Her room, on the third day,
Was found empty. She ran away.
No one did know
Where and how
She then did disappear.
But fisherman did hear
That night, a maiden's whisper,
And a Cossack's speech, a thud of horses,
And in the early morning, a trace of horseshoes
Eight were found on the dewy grass.

The first down of cheeks, the flaxen young curls,
Do not always win the love of a girl.

At times the old man's
Scars of countenance,
His gray hair,
Will the dreams of a maid ensnare.
Soon the news of his disgrace
Reached the ear of Kochubey.
She her honor did betray.
Maria was found in Mazepa's embrace!
What a shame! Father and mother, underhand
Disgraceful fame of gossip dare not understand.
Then, only, the truth appeared
And all things they did comprehend
In the behavior of the culprit:
Why willfully she disappeared,
Why she refused to be a bride,
Why secretly she pined and sighed,
Why always to the greeting of the grooms
With proud insolence she replied;
Why when at the table they did dine
While foaming was the wine,
She only heard
The Hetman's word,
And always sang a song
Composed by him,
While he was yet poor and young,
And gossip did not know him;
Why with non-feminine soul, always she did haunt
The military front,
And loved the drums' martial sound,
The cries and the blare
Before the Hetman's staff and saber.
Rich and powerful is Kochubey.
Many friends are his. If he chose
He could with blood his own disgrace wash away.
He could with steady hand slay
In his court; all Poltava he might arouse.
But another thought did sway
At the time the heart and mind of Kochubey.

It was then a seditious time in the land,
When Russia, young,
Straining her strength,
With the genius of Peter was growing strong.
A stern teacher in the science of glory
Was given to her, and not one
Lesson, bloody and admonitory
She received then from the Swedish throne;
But amidst temptations of the ordeal,
Crushed beneath fortune's heel,
Russia still at that time did ful- fill.
Thus a hammer crushing glass, is forging steel.
With a vain crown of glory on his proud brow,
Bold Charles glides along the precipice.
Is marching on the road to ancient Moscow.
And before him the Russian arm sweeps
Like a storm in its mightiness,
Bending dusty grass.
He marches on the same path
Where afterward there left his trace
Another man of fate, in our days,
And who, with his defeat glorified
His retreating flight.

Ukrania was filled with unrest.
Long the spark was fanned;
Devotees of her bloody glorious past
Proudly did demand
That Hetman their bond rend
With Russia. Their light-minded enravishment,
Impatiently awaited
Charles. Around Mazepa youth then agitated
For a war. But he remained to Peter obedient,
Keeping sternness habitual,
He calmly over Ukrania ruled.
It seemed all gossip he then scorned,
And but caroused unconcerned.

"What is vexing our Hetman?" youths complained.

"He is sick, he is old.
War and years his strength have drained.
No longer is he bold.
Why carry saber with trembling hand?
Why doth he submit to the foe?
Now is the fateful time with warlike storm to descend
Upon the hated Moscow.
If old Doroshenko,
If Samoilovitch, the young,
Paley of Gordeyenko,
Be ruling our military throng.
Cossacks would now not be dying
Amid the snows of distant lands;
The enemy within our Fatherland
They would be defying."

Thus for adventure burning,
Bold youth was yearning
For war. Dangerous changes were abetting,
Fatherland's prolonged captivity forgetting,
Bogdan's lucky arguments,
The Holy Wars, and past agreements.
Old age is stepping carefully,
Observes all suspiciously:
From what to refrain and what is right
To do, he doth not immediately decide.
But who would penetrate the depths of the seas
covered with immovable ice?
Who shall penetrate a deep abyss
And its depths there scrutinize?
His plans and his thought
Are but fruit of his suppressed vice.
Deeply beneath the surface they float.
The goal to which he applied
His artifice, he along descried.
Who knows? The more Mazepa is cruel,
The more lying and shrewder is his soul,
The more courteous he seems a friend.

He always knew, all powerful,
How the hearts of men to attract and understand,
And safely their minds to rule.
How shrewdly confident,
At feasts, with simple-minded grace
He conversed with the old men
As another gossiping old man
Yearning for the old glorious days.
With one self-willed, freedom he glorified;
Inveighed against authority with one dissatisfied;
With one embittered he was shedding tears;
With one unwise,
Discoursed with his sensible advice.
Not many understood
That his will was untamable;
That he ever did persecute
Adversaries by means dishonorable;
That all his life that he did live
Was never known an insult to forgive;
That far and wide
Reached out his criminal sight;
That he knew no sanctitude;
That he never knew gratitude;
That nothing in the world he prized;
That like water he was ever ready to shed blood;
That freedom he despised;
That no Fatherland he recognized.

For a long time, a dangerous plan
Nurtured the cruel man;
But his plan a hostile eye did penetrate,
And his intention did anticipate.
No audacious destroyer! No bird of prey!
Gnashing his teeth, mused Kochubey,
"My abode I will spare.
Thou wilt not die amid the glare
Of a fanned conflagration,
From a Cossack saber.
No murderer!

In the hand of the Moscow executioner
Thou wilt in thy torture deplore;
Thou wilt curse the day and hour
When thou baptized our child,
When a cup for thee I did pour
And that night
When thou pecked our dove, old kite."
There was a time when Kochubey's
Friend was Mazepa. In those days
As with salt and bread and ale
Their thoughts both did share;
From the field of glory often did hail,
Their horses side by side,—an unseparable pair.
Often then, the Hetman, in obscure ale,
Of a forthcoming betrayal,
Revolutions and negotiations,
Secret communications,
With him thus his thought did share,
His insatiable soul before him laid bare:
So true was Kochubey's
Heart to him in those days.
But now the mind of the embittered Kochubey
By one thought only is swayed.
He nourishes but one thought night and day:
"I will perish or conquer,
And avenge my child's odious dishonor."
Long, his enterprising rancor
Hidden in his heart he bore.
In impotent grief he directed
His thoughts to the grave.
No longer, he Mazepa's destruction craved.
"My daughter guilty," he reflected;
But even his own daughter he did forgive;—
Let her to God an answer give.
Such dishonor upon her family to bestow,
Unmindful of heaven and His law.

Meanwhile he scanned, with eagle eyes,
For partisans, to share his enter prise.

To his wife confidingly he dis-   closed
His mind. In the silence of the night
A letter was composed.
His wife, full of woman's spite,
Urged him on. Like an evil spirit
On bed of sleep she did entreat,
Whispering of vengeance and raging,
Shedding tears, encouraging,
And an oath did demand that her word he will obey.
And an oath gave her the somber Kochubey.

The blow was prepared.
Fearless Iskra their plans shared
With them. But who, burning with impassioned zeal
For the commonweal,
Would dare this letter of Kochubey
To take and at Tsar Peter's feet to lay?

Among the Poltava Cossacks was one
Who in the days by-gone,
Maria idolized,
And whom Maria hath despised.
Evening and morning hour
Along the banks of his native river,
In the shade of the wild cherries, for her
He often patiently was waiting.
He was consoled by a brief meeting;
Dared not to tire her with his entreating,
And it seemed a refusal he would not survive.
When grooms in crowds did arrive,
From their midst he fled.
When among the Cossacks suddenly
Maria's shame spread,
And gossip then unsparingly
With jeering struck her head,
Even then over him
Maria reigned supreme.
But if one, though accidently,
Before him uttered Mazepa's name,

Then suffering secretly
To earth he cast his eyes, ashamed.

Who beneath the moon and starry skies
So late at night doth ride?
Whose mettled horse in the distance flies
Over boundless steppe so wide?
Cossack to north is riding fast,
Cossack will not stay or rest,
At no crossing, not in field,
Nor in a grove concealed.

Like the glass his sword is glimmering
At his bosom gold doth ring.
The steed no false step on his way
Doth make. Flying, with his mane doth sway.

Gold he needs, the daring boy;
The sword is fun for the daring lad;
The mettled horse, is also joy'
But more precious is the hat.

To him the hat is more worth
Than horse, gold, and his sword.
He will part with his hat
Only in battle with shattered head.

Why is the hat so dear to him?
Because a letter is sewn in,
About the Hetman's treacherous way
To Tsar Peter from Kochubey.

Mazepa, meantime, in his plots was persisting;
Some Jesuit was meeting,
Planning an uprising;
A frail throne they were raising.
Under cover of night hiding,
They carry on negotiations;
Betrayals they are buying;
Composing the Hetman's proclamations;

Trade with the Tsar's head,—
An oath for the vassals they're contriving.
A beggar in the court doth tread,
No one knows from whence arriving.
Orlik, Hetman's shrewd assistant,
To secret missions is him sending.
Servants, by Mazepa sent,
Everywhere poison are implanting.
With Bultan they are muddling
Among the Cossack hordes on the river Don.
Rekindling their ardor of days by-gone,
Behind the rapids of the Dnieper
They scare the violent throng
With the autocracy of Peter.
Mazepa everywhere his net hath flung,
And many letters sends to different lands.
With crafty menace doth array
Upon Moscow, Bakhchisaray.
The king in Warsaw his advice obeys,
And in Ochakov, Pascha's grace,
In his camp, Charles and the Tsar are seen.
One thought another doth awaken;
His cruel will doth not weaken
In him. His crafty soul doth not sleep in him;
More securely he's preparing his blow.
Tireless is the ardor of the foe.
But how he bestirred
When suddenly he heard,
Like a thunder, a sudden blow,
When to him the foe
Of Russia, the grandees of Moscow
Turned over the letter of accusation.
But instead of a well-warranted investigation
Kindness on him, as though upon a victim
They bestowed.
The Tsar himself his faith in Judas hath avowed;
And promised him his foe's hate
With befitting punishment he will cause to abate.

Preoccupied with the cares of war,
The Tsar apparent slander did abhor.
And to Kochubey's accusations he paid no attention.
Mazepa then to the Tsar raised his voice
With humble pretention:
"God knows, and the world is aware
That he, poor Hetman, twenty years did serve
Faithfully the Tsar with utmost care,
From path of duty did not swerve.
By the Tsar to glory he was raised,
For his labor amply was repaid.
And how blind is hate!
Doth it befit him at the end of his days
Nor to begin a study of new ways
Of betrayal, and his glorious name
With thankless treachery to defame?
Doth not the Tsar know
That he a crown of Ukrainia did reject,
And all agreements and letters, as he would expect
From his faithful subject
To him, Tsar he did direct?
Was not he to the instigations of the Khan
And the Constantinople Sultan,
Remain unmoved? Burning with zeal
For his country's weal,
Was he not ever ready his land to defend?
With his mind and saber
With the foes of the Tsar to contend?
Neither labor nor life did he spare;
And now how doth a hateful foe dare
His gray hair to cover with shame,
And his glorious name to defame?
And who are they?
His life-long friends—Iskra and Kochubey!"
With cold-blood audacity,
With tears blood-thirsty
He for execution to the Tsar prays.
Whose execution?—stubborn old man!—

Whose daughter is in they embrace?
Cold is the heart of a cruel man;
He thinks: Why did he, madman,
Begin this unequal squabble?
His own daring scheme
Sharpened the axe for him.
Where, with eyes closed, did he race?
Upon what did he his hopes base?
Or....But daughter's love will never save
Her father from the grave.
No!—or my own blood will flow!

Maria, poor Maria awake!
Thou knowest not what a treacherous snake
Upon they breasts thou art caressing,
What depraved power is thee obsessing?
What cruel soul thee enticed?
To whom wert thou made a sacrifice?
Mazepa's gray hair, his sunken, flashing eyes,
Above all on earth thou dost prize.
With his quiet speech
He hath thee betwitched.
For thy bed with seduction spread
Thy father and thy mother thou didst forget.
With crafty speech thy conscience
He lulled to sleep. Thy countenance
Thou turnest to him with veneration.
Thou dost cherish him with touching admiration.
To thee, is enjoyable thy shame,
And with it, as with chastity dost boast
The tender beauty of thy purity
In thy fall thou hath lost.
What is shame to Maria?
What matters to her the gossip of the folk?
What is to her, people's talk?
Upon her breasts rests the old man's proud head.
When with her, the Hetman doth forget
His fortune, his laborious care.

The terrible secrets of his daring ways
To her, a timid maid, he lays bare.
She is not sorry for the innocent days.
Only one affliction upon her soul
At times like a passing cloud strays.
Father, mother, sorrowful,
Before her she portrays.
She sees them through her tears,
Sorrow in their childless old age they bear,
It seems as though their complaints she doth hear.
If only she knew
What all Ukrania doth expect....
But as yet she had no clue
To the shameful secret.

PART II.

Mazepa is somber. A cruel plan
His confused mind dreams.
Maria on her old man
With tender eyes beams.
At his knees she sits
And words of love repeats,
n vain: From his mind her love
Would not anxiety remove.
Distracted, to the earth
He directs his glance,
And Maria's tender words
He greets with silence.
Insulted, surprised,
Scarcely breathing, she doth rise
From her place to him makes her plea:
"Listen, Hetman, for thee
All things on earth I made a sacrifice.
But when to thee myself I did bind,
Only one thing I had in mind:
Thy love. and for its sake, my happiness
I ruined. Still for naught I now pine....
But remember in that terrible silence

When I became thine
Thou gavest an oath to love me.
and why dost thou not love me?"

Mazepa:
"My friend, forget thy frenzied dream.
Thou wilt thy heart but foolishly ruin.
Blind passion
Is agitating thee with unjust suspicion.
Maria, trust me,
More than power I prize thee."

Maria:
"'Tis not true. Thou art dealing craftily with me.
How long since thou wert inseparable from me?
Now from my caresses thou dost flee!
The whole day thou dost hide,
In the circle of elders, or somewhere thou dost ride
And I am forgotten. Thou alone all night dost sit
Either with the beggar or with the Jesuit.
All my love, timid,
But with cold harshness does meet.
Not long ago,
Thou drank, I know,
To the health of Lady Dulsky.
That's news! Who is that Lady Dulsky?"

Mazepa:
"What? Dost thou with jealousy rage?
Listen, doth it befit me at my age
To seek greetings haughty
From a self-indulgent beauty?
Will I, a stern man, my honor stain—
Like an idle youth myself disguise?
Will I consent to drag a shameful chain,
and with dissimulation men's wives entice?"

Maria:
"No; without reserve explain.
Talk simply, without restraint."

Mazepa:
"Thy peace of thy soul is dear to me,

Maria, so be it, I will confess to thee....

"Long we began an enterprise,
Our work prevailing doth appear.
A favorable time, I surmise,
The hour of a great struggle is near.
A long time our freedom we were not defending.
A long time our heads we were bending,
Beneath the protection of Warsaw,
under the autocracy of Moscow.
Now the time has arrived
At last for Ukrania to be a kingdom.
And against Peter I now connive.
Against him I raised the banner of our freedom.
Both kings with me negotiate.
And, perchance, amid the quarrels, I will create
The ambition which I conceived;
A throne for myself I will achieve.
I have friends, dependable,
Countess Dulsky, the Jesuit,
The beggar, all capable,
Supporting me to achieve my deed.
Important letters always they bring
To me from the king.
Thou hast attained my confession.
Art thou satisfied?
And thy unjust apprehension
Pray, was it justified?"
Maria:
"O, my friend,
Thou wilt be the Tsar of our land.
How thy gray hair is befitting
A crown of a king!"
Mazepa:
"Be patient. A storm will arise,
And who will surmise
What might become of me?"
Maria:
"I know no fear when I am near thee.

Thou art so powerful. I know
A crown Mazepa doth await."
Mazepa:
"And if it turn my fate
On the scaffold to go?"
Maria:
"I will then with thee to the scaffold go!
O! How could I survive thee?
But no!
The sign of power is upon thy brow!"
Mazepa:
"Dost thou love me?"
Maria:
"Do I love thee?"
Mazepa:
"Who is thee dearer,—
I, or thy father?"
Maria:
"Why dost thou question so relentlessly?
Why dost thou alarm me unnecessarily?
I endeavored to forget my family.
My father (what a terrible dream!)
Perchance I am now cursed by him.
Was it not all for the sake of thee?"
Mazepa:
"Then I am dearer to thee
Than thy father, as I understand....
Why art thou silent?"
Maria:
"O, God!"
Mazepa:
"So what?"
Maria:
"Decide for yourself."
Mazepa:
"Listen, if he or I needs must perish,
Only one of us to live,
And thou be the judge,

And it be for thee to choose,
To whom would thou thy protection give?"
Maria:
"Enough! Do not agitate my heart!
A tempter thou art!"
Mazepa:
"Answer!"
Maria:
"Thou art pale, and stern is thy speech.
Be not angry, I beseech.
Fearful are thy words to me.
Trust me.
All sacrifice for thy sake
I will ever be glad to make."
Mazepa:
"Remember, Maria, what thou hast said!"

Silent the Ukrainian night.
Transparent the sky; stars are bright.
To overcome its drowsiness, the air
Doth not care.
Hardly tremble dare
The leaves of silver poplars.
The moon silent, from its height,
Upon Bela-Tzerkov pours its light.
The gorgeous gardens and the old castle
'tis painting bright,
And quiet—quiet all around.
Only from the castle doth a voice resound.
In the turret, there with chains bound,
Beneath a window, Kochubey lies,
Thoughtful, somber, gazing at the skies.

Tomorrow on the scaffold he will appear,
But he doth not the horrible execution fear.
He is not sorry that his life expired.
What is death to him? A sleep but much desired....
He hath prepared himself to die,
In a blood-stained coffin to lie.

But upon God, the righteous, he doth call.
O, God! At the murderer's feet silently to fall,
Like a speechless creature,
From his hand endure torture,
To be turned over to his power
By the Tsar, to a traitor's breed,
To lose life and honor,
And his friends with him to the scaffold lead
And there to hear them curse and rave
Over his grave....
Innocent beneath the axe to lie
And meet the foe's joyful eye:
To lay down for eternal sleep,
And to no one, no one, his hate bequeath!

He then remembered his Poltava thoughtfully,
The usual circle of his family,
His past glory, riches, and his lands,
The songs of his daughter, his friends,
The house where he was born,
Where peacefully he oft in sleep did lie,
And all things that his life did adorn
And what willingly he threw away....
And for what?

The rusty key in the lock rings.
He wakes and the unfortunate thinks:
"Here beneath the banner of the cross is coming in,
On my bloody path, to me, a powerful guide,
The all-merciful absolver of my sin,
The spiritual comforter, the servant of Christ,
Who for the sake of all was crucified.
His blood and body to me he is bringing.
My enfeebled soul strengthening,
I will fearlessly approach the night;
And with eternal life I will unite."
With heart penitent,
Unfortunate Kochubey, with his soul bared,
Before the all-powerful, the Infinite,

His woe to pour out was prepared.
But not a holy hermit—
Another guest he recognized,—
Cruel Orlik he did meet.
Overwhelmed with disgust, thus the man despised
He bitterly did greet.
"Thou art here again, cruel slave?
Why to disturb my last night's lodging
Camest thou here, thou knave?

Orlik:
"Thou hast more questions to answer.
My work is not done."

Kochubey:
"Everything have I answered.
Leave me alone."

Orlik:
"More confessions the lordly Hetman
Doth demand."

Kochubey:
"Long ago I admitted all he desired.
I was crafty....I lied....
The Hetman was right.
What more doth he desire?"

Orlik:
"We know thou wert rich.
And many treasures beyond our reach
In Dikanka by thee are hidden.
To the scaffold tomorrow thou wilt proceed.
Thy fortune thou wilt cede
To the military treasure.
This is law. Reveal
Then where thy treasures are concealed."

Kochubey:
"Thou art right. Three treasures
In this life I enjoyed.
One treasure was my honor
Which this torture hath destroyed.
Another gone forevermore,

My daughter's honor.
I watched over it night and day.
This treasure Mazepa took away.
Only one treasure,—only vengeance I did save,
And this, to God Almighty, I carry with me
    to my grave."
Orlik:
"Old man, be not wroth,
Tomorrow thy soul wilt surrender.
Feed thyself on stern thought,—
No time to jest. Answer,
Lest another torture thou wilt invite.
Where didst thou thy money hide?"
Kochubey:
"Cruel, sneaking slave,
How long will I thy senseless words endure?
Suffer me to lie down in my grave,
Then go with Mazepa at thy pleasure
And count my treasure.
My cellars break open, my wealth acquire,
My houses and gardens set on fire;
My daughter will point to thee my riches.
Take her along!
But for God's sake, I beseech thee
Let me now alone."
Orlik:
"Where didst thou thy money hide?
Tell us outright:
Where is thy money—point the spot.
If not, a cruel lot
Be thine. Art thou silent?
Then on the rack we will torment
Thee....Hey—executioner!"

O cruel night of sufferance!
But where is the Hetman? Where is the murderer?
Where-to did he flee his conscience?
In the room of his admirer,

The sleeping maid yet blessed with ignorance,
Near the bed of his god-child, at her side
With bent head, somber, quiet,
He was sitting.
Thoughts in his mind were seething,
Each more somber than the other:
"He will die, the madman Kochubey.
I will not the execution stay.
The nearer the fateful day
Approaches, the sterner must be my power.
Enmity before me lower
And yet lower shall bend.
The informer and his assistant—
They will surely die."
But, casting his eye
Upon the bed, he thinks: "But what will become of her,
O, God, when she will discover
    that her father was slain?
She doth not know yet what awaits her.
But the secret will not remain
Long hidden. The sound of the axe at morning, falling
Over all Ukrania will be rolling.
And the talk of the people she will hear.
I see that one for life's commotion born
Fearlessly, alone should face the storm.
One fated for life's strife
Should never invite for himself a wife.
To one wagon 'tis impossible to rope
A horse and a timid antelope.
Thoughtless passion did sway
My mind. Now for my madness, I tribute pay.
Everything beyond all price
The maid to me hath made a sacrifice;
    and what woe, forsooth,
Did I for her prepare!"
He thinks: "How sweetly rests youth!
How tenderly for her sleep doth care!
How peacefully her breast heaves,

How calmly she breathes.
But tomorrow—heavens!—how will she the fateful
  news greet?"

Mazepa then his glance turned away;
And quietly making his way
Into the solitary garden did stray.

Quiet Ukrainian night,
Transparent the skies; stars are bright.
To overcome its drowsiness, the air
Doth not care.
Hardly tremble dare
Leaves of the silver poplars.
A somber, strange dream
Perturbed Mazepa's mind. The stars
Like accusing eyes upon him
Their glances are casting.
In rows, the poplars 'round him investing,
Among themselves like judges, protesting
And whispering seem,
Their heads shaking jeeringly at him;
And the summer darkness of the night
Like a dungeon his heart dos spite.

Suddenly a weak, long drawn lamentation
From the castle he doth hear.
Was it a dream of imagination?
A cry of fear?
A brute's howl? Torture's groan
Or some other moan?
Only his soul's conflict
Mazepa could no more restrict
And to the weal, long drawn voice,
He answered with another—that same sound
With which so wildly he did rejoice
  and with which the field of battle he made resound
When with Zabela, with Combeley,
And with him—that Kochubey—

Through the flame of battle
Galloping, he often made his way.

With its red streaks, the morning
Brightly the skies embraced.
The woods and meads adorning,
The waves of rivers with sunshine graced.
The noise of early morn was heard
Playfully above the earth.
Daylight broke, and man awoke.
Maria with dreams embraced
Heard how someone entered, on her gazed,
Silently her bed approached,
And her feet lightly touched.
Maria awoke; and her eyes did raise.
But quickly with a smile, her eyes again she closed
From the glare of the morning rays.
Still in her sleep calmly reposed,
Maria outstretched her hands,
Whispering with languishing indulgence:
"Mazepa, thou?" But heard another voice reply.
Trembling, she looked up and beheld
Her mother standing nigh....
Mother:
"Be quiet, be quiet!
Lest thou wilt ruin us. Tonight
I sneaked in cautiously,
On my lips one entreaty:
Only thou may stay their cruelty.
The execution is today.
Save thy father, Kochubey."
Daughter (In terror):
"What father?
What execution?"
Mother:
"Why? dost thou not know?
Not in a desert thou art!
Thou art in the court. Thou shouldst know
How cruel is the Hetman's heart,

How his foes he doth punish,
What power on him the Tsar doth lavish.
I see thy sorrowful family thou doth not mind.
For sake of Mazepa thou didst us renounce.
Thee I sleeping find
When the cruel sentence they announce,
When they sharpen the axe for thy father.
I see we are strangers to each other.
Bethink thyself, maria, daughter!
Be an angel to us.
Run! Mazepa find,
Fall on thy knees, pray.
Thy glance the murderer's hands will bind,
Thy word the cruel axe will stay.
Demand. Hetman will not refuse.
For his sake thy family thou didst renounce,
Thy honor forgot,
And God!"
Daughter:
"What is with me?
Father....Mazepa....Execution!
My mother her I find....
With prayer....It seems
I've lost my mind!
Or perchance
They're all fantasies....distorted dreams?"
Mother:
"God be with thee!
No. no. No fantasy, no dreams!
Dost thou not know
That thy father, hardened by the blow
Of his daughter's dishonor,
Desiring revenge evermore
Against Hetman, to the Tsar a letter sent?
That if God's powerful hand
Be not sparing, today on the scaffold he will stand
And before a military throng be executed?
And that now he is sitting here in the turret?"

Daughter:
"Today? O, father!
My poor father!"

And on the bed, the poor maid
Cold as a corpse was laid.
Seas of many-colored heads,
Spears are sparkling, glistening,
Drums are beating, Serdyuks are galloping,
In battle order regiments are forming.
Hearts are trembling. Throngs are humming.
On the wide road, like a snake's tail,
Crowds of people trail.
And in the center of the field
A fateful scaffold is built.
On it, rejoicing, promenading,
The executioner awaiting
The victims greedily.
In his white hand he is taking
The ponderous axe playfully,
Is jesting with the happy mob.
In one noisy sound merged all voices:
Women's cries, laughs, murmurs, curses....
Suddenly an exclamation!
And all hearts beat in silent trepidation;
In the deep silence, resounded
Over the field the horses' thud.
By his Serdyuks surrounded,
At a gallop the lordly Hetman rode
On a black horse.
And there on the Kiev road
The sight of a wagon rose.
Kochubey, supported by his powerful faith,
With heaven and earth his peace hath made.
And beside him, Iskra, quiet, indifferent,
Like a lamb submissive to his fate....
The wagon stopped.
The smoke of the censers rose....

The loud-voiced singers then prayed
For the soul's repose
Of the unfortunate....
Up the scaffold they go,
While multitudes in silent prayer bow....
Making the sign of the cross, Kochubey prayed,
And his head on the scaffold laid.
Silence over the field spread.
The axe flashed, and away sprang his head.
The whole field sighed.
Blinking, rolled another head
In the people's sight.
The grass with blood was painted red.
Happy in his heart, the executioner both
By the hair hath caught,
In his hands them took
And above the crowds the heads he shook.

The execution over, the mob unconcerned
To their homes were walking,
About their daily business talking.
Only then upon the many-colored road
Two dusty, tired women trod.
To the place of execution they were hurrying.

It seemed in great fear, sorrowing,
They were running. "Too late,"
With his finger pointing to the field
Someone to them said.
There the scaffold that was built,
Now they were breaking. In black vestments
  a priest prayed;
And two Cossacks upon a wagon
Were then raising an oaken coffin.

Alone, ahead of the throng mounted,
Stern Mazepa, from the place of execution rode away.
With a terrible void was he tormented.
No one came to meet him on his way.

His horse, covered with foam,
Was flying. Arriving home,
"How is Maria?" he asked, full of fear.
But dull and timid answers did he hear.
He entered her room.
Empty is the silent room.
In the garden he set out to roam;
Around the wide pond, the shrubs,
Along the peaceful shadows;
In no place
Could he find her trace.
Agile Serdyuks him escorting,
He did call. They run, their horses snorting.
The wild cry of chase
Was heard. Mounted, the braves did race
Full speed to every place.

The precious moments fly.
No one Maria did espy.
No one knew, no one could say
Where and how she ran away;
Unearthly rage Mazepa torments.
Trembling, silent, are his servants.
In her room himself he did hide,—
In her room all night,
He did abide with open eyes.
As the morn the skies set a-flame,
Each messenger to his palace came.
Saddles girth, horseshoes, bridles,
Scattered, broken, covered with flood and foam;
But no one returning home
A trace of the poor maid found.
She disappeared like an empty sound.
Only the mother
Stricken with the fatal blow,
Into exile carried away with her
Her poverty and her woe.

PART III.

Affliction's consuming fire
Did not prevent Ukrania's
Ambitious ruler to his goal to aspire.
Relentlessly pursuing his designs,
With Charles he continued negotiations,
But more certain to prevent
Suspicion of unfriendly accusation,
Suffering on sick bed he doth pretend.
He is cared for by a throng of physicians,
The fruits of war, labor, and of his passions,
Affliction, sickness, submissive he doth endure.
Plaintively Mazepa is sighing for a cure.
Foreboding of approaching death
Hath chained him to his bed.
Fearing his life expires,
To perform the holy ceremony he desires.
The Prelate is going
For the death-bed him to prepare.
On his crafty gray hair
Holy unction is flowing.

Time is flowing. Moscow in vain
Hourly the Swedes is awaiting;
At a secret solemnity anticipating
The guests to entertain.
Suddenly Charles turned back
To Ukrania. His war thence he carried.
The day arrived, and this human wreck,
Mazepa, left his death-bed;
Who but yesterday
Was sighing for his grave
Today he is Peter's adversary brave.
Before the regiments he's brandishing his saber,
His proud eyes flare.
To Densa he goes
Flying on his horse.
Like that crafty cardinal, bent with strenuous life

When with Roman tiara he was crowned,
Again he's powerful, youthful and alive.

The news on wings was broadcast.
Ukrania, confused, did agitate:
"He went over, he betrayed.
At Charles' feet he laid
Down his submissive staff."
The fanned flame yet more extensive grows.
The bloody dawn of a people's war rose.
What scribe dare the rage of the Tsar describe?
Anathemas thunder in the churches.
Mazepa's effigy tortures
The executioner. At a noisy meeting
Cossacks a newly-elected Hetman are greeting
From the desert shores of Enisey.
The families of Iskra and Kochubey
To the Tsar's camp are speeding.
He is with the, tears shedding, with words of solace
   greeting.
Upon them he lavishes
New honors and new riches.
The foe of Mazepa, the old man Paley
From the darkness of exile, from afar,
Into the camp of the Tsar
Is making his way.

On the scaffold perishes
Chechel, fearless,
And the Zaporezshian Ataman;
And thou, the lover of military fame,
Who for a helmet flung thy crown,
Thy hour, too, came.
From in the distance, the sight
Of Poltava's ramparts thou espied.

And the Tsar, thence,
His hosts sends;
And they like a storm, came a-bounding;

Amid the plain, both camps
Craftily each other are surrounding.
Thus oft bruised in daring combat,
Drunk with blood beforehand,
A formidable champion at last
Meets the other, breast to breast;
And enraged, powerful Charles sees
No confused clouds of Narva's fugitives,
But a line of well-ordered regiments,
Calm, glittering, obedient,
And walls of firm bayonets.
And he decided: tomorrow to war he intends.
Profound sleep amid the Swedish tents;
Only in one, where
Two are conversing in a whisper.

"No, Orlik, No, my lad.
We acted in haste, and at an ill moment.
My plan was audacious and bad.
No good will come from it.
I lost my goal, evidently,
I seemed to miss my aim badly.
In that Charles, I erred.
True he is a bold and daring lad.
Two, three battles might I successfully contest;
He may arrive galloping at the adversary's repast.
A bomb he will greet with a jest.
No, worse than a Russian sharpshooter, he may
Steal into the foe's camp, and perchance,
Drop a Cossack like today,
And a wound for a wound he can exchange.
But not for him to contend
With the autocratic giant.
He aspires, as with a drum, a regiment,
To compel fate in circles to turn about.
He is blind, stubborn and impatient,
Light-minded and proud.
Whose star to trust, but God knows.
He will break his horns.

The enemy's new strength
According his first success, he doth represent.
His daring ventures, I find,
Made me blind.
I am ashamed. A military tramp did me infatuate
At my age, like a timid maid."
Orlik:
"Let us wait. 'Tis not too late
With Peter again to negotiate.
We may mend the break.
Defeated, the Tsar surely will not refuse
Peace with us to make."
Mazepa:
"No, 'tis late.
Our break is irrevocable.
With the Russian Tsar it is impossible
For me to make peace. His fate
Long ago I did decide.

In my breast. Once near Azov, in the Tsar's tent,
Carousing, a night I spent.
With wine our cups were stirred,
And stirred speeches it aroused.
I uttered a reckless word.
The youthful guests were all confused.
The Tsar then lighted,
Dropped his cup, excited.
My moustache he grasped threatening.
With impotent rage then to him submitting,
An oath of vengeance that day I did utter.
Deeply in my heart I buried it,
And like a mother
In her womb a child, I carried it.
The time arrived. He will remember me to
  the very end
Of his days. To Peter I was sent
As punishment.
He will part with many an hour

Of his life, and many cities old,
That he may again, as of yore,
Mazepa by his moustache hold.
Yet there is still hope in sight....
Who of us will be put to flight,
The morrow's morn will decide."
He ceased to speak and closed his eyes;
Silence hence, reigned supreme over the camp
   that night.

In the east a new day woke.
From the hills and over the valleys
Guns thundered. Red smoke,
To meet the morning rays,
Rose to the skies in rings.
The regiments closed ranks.
Sharpshooters behind the shrubs are crawling.
Bullets whistling, cannonballs rolling,
Cold bayonets are jutting.
The Swedes, beloved sons of victory,
Through the fire are strutting.
Agitated, flies the cavalry.
Behind them slowly moves the infantry.
And cavalry's intrepidity
Is strengthening with its solidity.
The fateful battlefield
Rumbles. Here and there 'tis burning,
Apparently the God of War doth us shield.
Warlike fortune the Russians is serving.
By the fire beaten back, the hosts
Retire, falling into dust.
Rosen is retreating down the steeps.
Ardent Schlipenback surrenders.
Column after column, we press the Swedes.
Darkened are the glory of their banners.
Apparently the God of War his blessing to us
   hath sent;
And with it, each of our steps is stamped.

Then by heaven inspired, jubilant,
The voice of Peter resounded:
"To our work, with God's help!" From his tent
By throngs of favorites surrounded
He comes out. His eyes are gleeful,
His face is stern.
He is beautiful.
He is like God's storm.
To him is brought his horse.
Obedient, the faithful horse
The fateful fire scenting,
He is trembling, his eyes are squinting,
And flies through the field's fire,
Proud of his sovereign rider.

Mid-day was near. The hot sun the plain was warming,
Like a ploughman the field was resting.
Regiments were lining up, reforming.
Here and there the Cossacks were molesting.
Upon the hills, the cannons their hungry howl tamed.
Suddenly with enthusiasm inflamed,
Resounded the whole plain.
The distance the shouts reechoes again,
"Hurrah!"
The regiments
Of Peter caught a glimpse.

Before his army he galloped by,
Happy, powerful like the war,
The field he devoured with his eye.
And behind him were riding fast
The birds of Peter's nest.
Through all fortune's changes on this earth
Sharing his labor, of government and war,
Sherematev of noble birth,
Pepin, Bruss and Boyer
And fortune's favorite, the orphan,
The semi-autocratic sovereign—and man.

Before the blue line
Of his military hosts, Charles, supine,
Suffering from his wound,
Was carried around.
His chieftains followed him.
Thoughtful, quiet, he seemed....
Yet his countenance anxiety expressed.
Charles, it seemed, the desired battle hath perplexed.
Suddenly, with a weak movement of his hands,
Upon the Russians he moved his regiments.

And with these, the Tsar's host met in the plain,
And the battle thundered a-main,
The battle of Poltava!
Beneath an incandescent rain
Repulsed by a live wall, in vain,
One fallen line another followed.
Bayonets closed. Like a heavy cloud
The flying cavalry was flanking,
With bridles and sabers clanking;
Each other into dust were dropping;
Straight from the shoulder they were chopping;
Heaps of bodies upon each other falling.
Castiron balls everywhere were rolling,
Bounding, the dust heaving
Or hissing in blood.
Swedes and Russians were cleaving,
Gnashing their teeth. Everywhere horses thud,
Howls of drums, thunder of guns,
Death, hell and groans.

Amid anxiety and agitation
On the field with eyes of inspiration,
Calmly the chieftains glance,
Watching movements of the regiments,
Forseeing victory's jubilation.
They were quietly conducting their conversation.
But who was this gray-haired warrior escorted
By two Cossacks, in his weakness supported

Who near the Moscow Tsar, the field
With experienced eye of a hero did behold?
In exile grown old,
Decrepit, gray,
No longer will he a horse ride,
And Cossacks on the call of Paley,
No longer will come flying from each side.
But why on a sudden flashed his glance,
And rage, like the darkness of the night,
Hath covered his countenance?
What possibly could him excite?
Perchance through the smoke he descried
His foe, Mazepa, and to hate
He began, this disarmed old man,
His age, and cruel fate?

Mazepa the battle field then scanned.
Over the field he pondered,
by the seditious Cossacks he was surrounded;
By his relatives, Serdyuks, chieftains,
Suddenly a shot. In Boynarovsky's hands,
From the musket, rings of smoke did ascend,
And at a few paces distance,
A young Cossack was in blood lying.
His horse scenting freedom,
Into the fiery distance was flying,
Covered with foam.
The Hetman approached him, riding,
And was talking while the Cossack he eyed.
But the Cossack, though dying,
With dimmed eyes was yet defying
The foe of Russia; his tongue hardly lisping,
Maria's tender name he was whispering.
Upon the Hetman, with saber in hand,
With mad rage in his eyes he did descend....

But our victory is near. Hurrah!
The Swedes are giving way.
One more attack. The foe is fleeing. We are

them crushing!
After them in mad pursuit, the cavalry is rushing.
Murder the swords is dulling;
And in one instant
The steppe is covered with bodies falling
Into dust
As swarms of black locusts.
Peter caroused.
Proud and serene
Full of glory his eyes beam.
Amid the shouts of his hosts, beautiful and grand
Was the Tsar's banquet.
In his tent he entertains
His own and the foreign chieftains.
The glorious captives he praises
And for his teachers a toast-cup raises.

But where is our first invited guest?
Where is our stern chief instructor
Whose lasting cruelty at last
Was subdued by the Poltava victor?
Where is Mazepa? Where is the murderer?
Where did Judas disappear
In fear?
Where is the Swedish king bold?
Why is not the traitor on the scaffold?

Over deserted steppe, mounted on their horses,
King and Hetman were flying on their course.
Fate forever bound them together.
Close danger and rancor
On the king great strength confer.
Mindless of his serious wound, he bounded
Over the plain, by the Russians hounded,
And his throng of faithful servants
Could scarcely keep abreast of him.

Surveying with his far-reaching sight,
The semi-circle of the steppe wide,

At the side of the king, Mazepa did ride.
Before him rose the sight of a house.
But what, suddenly, did the Hetman arouse?
Why, suddenly full of fright,
Full speed from the place he rode aside?

Hath this neglected court,
This house, this garden flowery,
The unlocked door to the world
Some old memory
To him recalled?
Seducer of holy innocence,
Hast thou recognized this habitance?
This home, once a happy home,
Where wine thou drank, and repasted,
And by the happy family surrounded,
At the table often jested?
Hast thou recognized this shelter modest
Which a peaceful angel did invest,
And the garden where beneath the open skies
Thou led her out into the steppes at night?
He did recognize! He did recognize!

The shadows of the night the steppe embrace.
On the bank of the blue Dnieper,
Amid the cliffs, in a somber, solitary place,
Slumber the foes of Russia, the foes of Peter.
Dreams spare the hero's rest,
He already the loss of Poltava forgot.
Not so is Mazepa's lot.
His somber spirit doth not rest
In him. Suddenly, amid the night's silence
He hears one call him. Awakening
He beholds a woman over him bends,
With her finger she is beckoning.
He trembles, as if beneath an axe he lies.
Upon him, with uncurled hair,
And glaring with sunken eyes,
Pale, in rags, she doth stare....

Suddenly she is lighted by the moon. And who?
"Is it a dream? Maria, is it possible—thou?
Maria:
"Silence, my friend! Just now mother and father
  did close their eyes; they may find us."
Mazepa:
"Maria, poor Maria!
Bethink thyself. What is with thee?"
Maria:
"Listen! What a funny story she told me!
She told me a secret,
That poor father died,
And silently she showed to me the sight
Of a gray-haired head.
O, God! How shall I from gossip hide?
Just think....This head
Was not a human head,
But a wolf's....
See....How she is!
How she tried to deceive me!
Is it not a shame thus to torture me?
And why? That I did not dare
Today to flee with thee!
Is that fair?"

With deep affliction the stern lover heard her.
But a tempest of thoughts carried her away.
"Still," she did say,
"I remember a noisy holiday,
And the mob....and two dead bodies,
Mother leading me to the celebration.
Where wert thou? Why this separation?
Let's go home. Hurry. It is late!
Oh, I see, am empty thought my mind doth agitate.
I mistook thee for someone....
Someone....O, leave me alone.
Thy glance is jeering, terrible.
Thou art ugly....He was beautiful!

In his eyes such loveliness,
In his speech such tenderness!
His moustache like the snow was white,
But on thine....Blood hath dried."

Suddenly she laughed and cried;
And like a young antelope, light,
She leaped off, and herself did hide
In the darkness of the night.

The shadows of the night were thinning;
The east was reddening.
A Cossack's fire in the steppe was flaring;
The Cossacks were a meal preparing.
The bodyguards to the Dnieper shores,
Their horses to water were leading.
"'Tis time," Charles arose.
"Arise, Mazepa, daylight is spreading."
But long, Mazepa was not sleeping.
Mortal anguish was eating
Him. In his breast his breathing
Was constrained; grim, seeming
Silent, his steed he was saddling,
And beside the runaway king was galloping,
And horribly his glance was gleaming,
While his native country he was leaving.
What now remains
With us of these proud men, today?
Their generation passed away.
And with them disappeared the bloody stains
Of their crime, victory and their misfortune.
Among the citizens of our north land
In the annals of our military fortune
Only thou, for thyself erected a monument:
Poltava's victory crowned.
In a country where many groups
Of winged mills with peaceful fence surround
Bender's desert slopes,
Where many a horned buffalo strays

Among the military graves,
The ruins of a vestibule are found:
Three holes in the ground,
Steps with moss overgrown,
Remind one here of the crowned
Swedish king. Here he was beating back
Alone with his own servants, one defender
Of the Turkish troops, a noisy attack,
And dropped his sword beneath the Turkish banner.

But in vain a mournful guest
Be searching for the grave where
  the Hetman doth rest.
Long since all trace of him did disappear.
Only once a year,
Solemnizing in a sanctity,
His anathema one doth hear.
But preserved is for us the grave
Where the martyrs rested.
Amid ancient holy graves
The church hath peacefully them sheltered.

In Dikanka many a row
Of oaks, planted by their friends, where grow.
To their children they relate
Of their executed grandfather's fate.
But the criminal daughter....Tradition
About her is silent. Her affliction,
The mystery of her end and fate,
No one yet did penetrate.
Only at times, a blind singer,
Before the people singing,
While the songs about Mazepa tinkling,
Of the sinful maiden's fate, on the sly,
To Cossack maidens, at times, doth testify.